Diane Warner's
Complete Book of

Revised Edition

D0958327

Diane Warner's
Complete Book of

Wedding Vows

Revised Edition

Hundreds of Ways to Say
"I Do!"

NEW PAGE BOOKS
A division of The Career Press, Inc.
Franklin Lakes, NJ

DIANE WARNER'S COMPLETE BOOK OF WEDDING VOWS, REV. ED.
EDITED AND TYPESET BY ASTRID DERIDDER
Cover design by DesignConcept
Printed in the U.S.A. by Book-mart Press

To order this title, please call toll-free 1-800-CAREER-1 (NJ and Canada: 201-848-0310) to order using VISA or MasterCard, or for further information on books from Career Press.

The Career Press, Inc., 3 Tice Road, PO Box 687,
Franklin Lakes, NJ 07417
www.careerpress.com
www.newpagebooks.com

Library of Congress Cataloging-in-Publication Data
Warner, Diane
  Complete book of wedding vows
  Diane Warner's complete book of wedding vows : hundreds of ways to say "I do" / Diane Warner. — Rev. ed.
      p.cm.
  Includes bibliographical references and index.
  ISBN 156414-816-5 (pbk.)
      1. Marriage service. I. Warner, Diane. Complete book of wedding vows. II. Title.

BL619.M37W37 2006
392.5—dc22

2005050474

With love to my granddaughter,
Renée.

Acknowledgments

My thanks go to all of those who shared their vows with me for this book, including hundreds of newlyweds and dozens of ministers, priests, and rabbis. I would especially like to thank the Reverend Father John Magoulias of the Greek Orthodox Church, Dr. John E. Stensether of the Evangelical Free Church of America, and Rabbi Stuart Dauermann of the Ahavat Zion Messianic Synagogue. I would also like to thank my daughter, Lynn Paden, as well as my friend, Helen Christy, who took their valuable time to help me with the monumental task of collecting wedding vows. An extra special thanks go to those couples who not only shared their vows, but their love stories as well: Andrew and Karen Goldberg; Ben and Wendi King; Joel and Colleen Blomenkamp; Joseph and Kathleen McLaughlin; Eric Wood and Kim Gray; Warren and Verna Riopel; Bill and Kathy Moran; Loren and Erma Hosmer; and my son and daughter-in-law, Darren and Lisa Warner.

Special thanks to my editor, Astrid deRidder, who worked so hard on this new edition.

ℰONTENTS

INTRODUCTION   11

CHAPTER ONE
Traditional vows   17

CHAPTER TWO
Nontraditional vows   33

CHAPTER THREE
Vows for second marriages   57

CHAPTER FOUR
Vows that include children   69

CHAPTER FIVE
Reaffirmation vows   79

CHAPTER SIX
Vows for older couples   97

CHAPTER SEVEN
   Vows with religious variations   105

CHAPTER EIGHT
   Ring vows   131

CHAPTER NINE
   Vows inspired by the classics   149

CHAPTER TEN
   Theme wedding vows   177

CHAPTER ELEVEN
   Original vows   197

EPILOGUE   203

BIBLIOGRAPHY   205

ALSO BY DIANE WARNER   209

INDEX   213

ABOUT THE AUTHOR   219

NTRODUCTION

The essence of every wedding is in the recitation of the vows. Without the vows themselves, the wedding day would be nothing more than a big party, a celebration of the couple's love for each other. The bride may be radiant as she glides down the aisle in her expensive designer gown, the massive cathedral may be opulently decorated from floor to rafters, and the professional musicians may bring tears to the eyes of your guests. But without the wedding vows, it is all just a silly waste of time and money.

Wedding vows have not always been part of the marriage ceremony, however. As we look back into history we find all manner of ways to marry. Many ancient cultures, including the Greeks, Romans, Jews, Medes, and Persians, used arranged marriages as a matter of practicality and common sense. The concept of romantic love had no part in these marriages, which were arranged for legal, financial, and social reasons, and only rarely did the ceremonies have any religious significance.

Those of you who love historical romance novels have probably chuckled at the barbaric methods of "marriage by capture," and it may seem as if this was something from the long distant past. However, marriage by capture was still legal in England until the 13th century! In some provinces of India, a Kanjar groom would gather his friends and arm them with muskets, stones, and sticks, and then descend on the home of his chosen bride. The families would fight until the bride's family finally surrendered her to the Kanjar groom.

And then there are the stories of the Australasian tribesmen who "married" the maidens of their choice by simply shooting barbless arrows through their legs.

Even the early Christians did not give marriage any religious significance until about the year 537 (common era). The Roman Catholic Church did not make marriage an official religious ceremony until the Council of Trent in 1563.

The American wedding of today, however, evolved from two great civilizations, Roman and Greek, where the bride wore a veil and the couple ate a special cake. The ceremony vows, as we know them today, emanated from the early Roman wedding. The Roman bride stood in her wedding costume, which consisted of a hemless tunic tied by a woolen girdle around her waist, fastened with a special knot called the Knot of Hercules. Over this tunic she wore a yellow cloak that matched her yellow sandals, and around her neck she wore a metal necklace. Over all of this she added a veil of red or yellow. On the crown of her head she wore a wreath of myrtle and orange blossoms. Finally, when she was thoroughly dressed, she stood with her family and welcomed her groom. At this point an animal was sacrificed (usually a sheep or a pig,) after which the couple joined hands and stood before a *pronuba*, a Roman priestess, where they publicly pledged themselves to each other. This was quite possibly the first official recitation of the wedding vow.

Wedding vows were also mentioned in the Bible; Hebrews 13:4 exhorts us to honor our marriage and its vows. But today, the wedding vow has become the *heart* of the marriage ceremony. In fact, it is said to be the highest vow known to mankind.

Throughout American history the wording of wedding vows was quite traditional, carefully treasured, and faithfully preserved by ministers, priests, and rabbis. Whenever these clergymen were called on to perform a wedding, the bride and groom accepted the traditional wording without question. It wasn't until the 1950s and 1960s (especially during the era of the barefooted flower children who took the formal marriage ceremony out of the sanctuary and onto the hillsides) that wedding vows began to evolve from the traditional to the nontraditional. In fact, most modern couples personalize their vows, composing them to express their deep feelings of love and commitment to one another.

This book offers the formal, traditional wedding vows, along with hundreds of personalized, nontraditional vows, including those used in second marriages, ceremonies of reaffirmation, marriages of older couples, and weddings involving children from previous marriages.

There are also chapters that offer vows with religious variations, vows inspired by the classics, and one devoted solely to ring vows. There are two new chapters included in this edition: Theme Wedding Vows and Original Wedding Vows. And just for fun, I've also sprinkled a few "up close and personal" love stories through-out the book that not only include the couples' personalized vows, but how they met and fell in love.

As you read through my *Complete Book of Wedding Vows*, you'll find that today's vows are written in three very different ways:

❖ Question-answer format.

❖ Monologue format.

❖ The very popular dialogue format.

As you consider the vows offered in this book, you may select one of them as your own, or you may, as the majority of couples do, use them to inspire you to write your own unique vows to each other. Some of the vows contain personalized references to the couple's history, physical features, or personalities. You should feel free to change the wording to fit you and your loved one.

Because this book contains the largest compilation of vows ever assembled, it should be read slowly and savored thoughtfully. It may help if you highlight the words, phrases, or complete vow segments you especially like as you read along.

This will make it easier for you to choose your favorite vow or to create your own. You'll see what I mean as you're reading along and certain phrases just seem to click as you say to yourself, "Yes! That's exactly the way I feel in my heart."

I want your wedding to be special! Bless you as you plan it and especially as you write your vows, the most important and precious part of your ceremony.

CHAPTER ONE
TRADITIONAL VOWS

Throughout history, traditional wedding vows have been structured out of time-honored societal and religious values. As recently as the 1950s, brides and grooms were willing to accept these traditional vows without question. In a sense, they willingly surrendered their union to the care and approbation of the larger community. This chapter gives many of these traditional vow phrasings from various faiths and nationalities.

> *In 1840, Queen Victoria wore a white wedding gown when she married Prince Albert. A few years later, French Empress Eugenie wore a white gown when she married Napoleon III. This was the beginning of the white dress tradition.*

Jewish

No single set of rules applies to all Jewish weddings because of differences between the Orthodox, Conservative, and Reform branches of the faith. In fact, most individual rabbis and synagogues develop their own interpretations. In the Orthodox and Conservative wedding services, an ancient Aramaic vow is usually recited before the groom places the ring on his bride's finger. This ring vow also serves as the groom's wedding vow. In the Sephardic transliteration, it reads:

17

"Harey at mekuddeshet li B'taba'at zo k'dat Moshe V'israel."

which means:

"Behold thou are consecrated unto me with this ring according to the law of Moses and of Israel."

In a double-ring ceremony, the bride presents a ring to her groom in the same way, reciting a slightly different vow.

During a Conservative service, these vows are often used, as taken from the Rabbinical Assembly Manual and published by the Rabbinical Assembly of America:

Rabbi (addressing the bridegroom): *"Do you, _____, take _____ to be your lawful wedded wife, to love, to honor and to cherish?"*

Groom: *"I do."*

Rabbi (addressing the bride): *"Do you, _____, take _____ to be your lawful wedded husband to love, to honor and to cherish?"*

Bride: *"I do."*

Rabbi (addressing the groom): *"Then, _____, put this ring upon the finger of your bride and say to her: 'Be thou consecrated to me, as my wife, by this ring, according to the Law of Moses and of Israel.'"*

The Rabbi then asks the bride to repeat the following:

"May this ring I receive from thee be a token of my having become thy wife according to the Law of Moses and of Israel."

If two rings are used, the bride may say:

"This ring is a symbol that thou art my husband in accordance with the Law of Moses and Israel."

In a Reformed service there is a distinctly separate wedding vow that is read by the rabbi and affirmed by both the bride and the groom:

"O God, supremely blessed, supreme in might and glory, guide and bless this groom and bride. Standing here in the presence of God, the Guardian of the home, ready to enter into the bond of wedlock, answer in the fear of God, and in the hearing of those assembled:

Do you, _____, of your own free will and consent, take this man/woman to be your wife/husband, and do you promise to love, honor, and cherish her/him throughout life?"

Groom/bride: *"I do."*

Reciting the Seven Blessings is also a traditional part of any Jewish marriage ceremony:

"You Abound in Blessings, Adonai our God, who created the fruit of the vine.

"You Abound in Blessings, Adonai our God. You created all things for Your glory.

"You Abound in Blessings, Adonai our God. You created humanity.

"You Abound in Blessings, Adonai our God. You made human-kind in Your image, after Your likeness, and You prepared from us a perpetual relationship. You abound in Blessings, Adonai our God. You created humanity.

"May she who was barren rejoice when her children are united in her midst in joy. You Abound in Blessings, Adonai our God, who makes Zion rejoice with her children.

"You make these beloved companions greatly rejoice even as You rejoiced in Your creation in the Garden of Eden as of old. You Abound in Blessings, Adonai our God, who makes the bridegroom and bride to rejoice.

"You Abound in Blessings, Adonai our God, who created joy and gladness, bridegroom and bride, mirth and exultation, pleasure and delight, love, fellowship, peace, and friendship. Soon may there be heard in the cities of Judah and in the streets of Jerusalem, the voice of joy and gladness, the voice of the bridegroom and the voice of the bride, the jubilant voice of bridegrooms from their canopies and of youths from their feasts of song. You Abound in Blessings, Adonai our God. You make the bridegroom rejoice with the bride."

Roman Catholic

The Roman Catholic Church follows strict doctrinal traditions, including those pertaining to the marriage ceremony. Although adherence to these traditions may vary slightly according to each individual parish priest's interpretation, there is usually very little deviation from tradition. This is especially true when the vows are recited during a wedding mass. Here are two examples of generally acceptable vow phrasings:

"I, _____, take you, _____, for my lawful wife/
husband, to have and to hold, from this day forward, for better, for
worse, for richer, for poorer, in sickness and health, until death do
us part."

or:

"I, _____, take you, _____, to be my husband/wife.
I promise to be true to you in good times and in bad, in sickness
and in health. I will love and honor you all the days of my life."

Eastern Orthodox

The churches of the Eastern Rite (including Greek and Russian
Orthodox) are similar in some ways to the Roman Catholic
Church. The marriage ceremony itself is a long ceremony rich
with symbolism. An Orthodox wedding begins with a betrothal
ritual that includes the Blessing and Exchange of Rings. The rings
are exchanged between bride and groom three times to signify
the Holy Trinity. At the close of this betrothal ritual, there is the
Marriage Rite, including the Candles and the Joining of Hands,
followed by the Crowning, the Cup and, finally, the Triumphal
Procession of Isaiah. The vows themselves are spoken silently
during this service, but the couple is considered married when
the crowns are finally removed by the priest and he blesses them
by saying:

"Be thou magnified,
O bridegroom."

> At a Dutch wedding, the bride's
> cake is often topped with a windmill,
> and the groom's cake is topped with
> a pair of wooden shoes.

Islam

It is forbidden for a Muslim woman to marry a non-Muslim man. A Muslim man however, may marry a non-Muslim woman. A traditional Muslim wedding requires a formal betrothal to take place, followed by the signing of the marriage contract, and then the wedding ceremony itself, where these vows are spoken:

Bride: *"I, _____, offer you myself in marriage in accordance with the instructions of the Holy Qur'an and the Holy Prophet, peace and blessing be upon Him. I pledge, in honesty and with sincerity, to be for you an obedient and faithful wife."*

Groom: *"I pledge, in honesty and sincerity, to be for you a faithful and helpful husband."*

Hindu

Hinduism is a religion native to India, broadly characterized by—among others—beliefs in reincarnation, a supreme being with many forms and natures, and a desire for liberation from earthly evils. Here is a modern-day interpretation of the traditionally strict Hindu wedding vows:

"Let us take the first steps to provide for our household a nourishing and pure diet, avoiding those foods injurious to healthy living. Let us take the second step to develop physical, mental, and spiritual powers. Let us take the third step, to increase our wealth by righteous means and proper use. Let us take the fourth step, to acquire knowledge, happiness, and harmony by mutual love and trust. Let us take the fifth step, so that we be blessed with strong, virtuous, and heroic children. Let us take the sixth step, for self-restraint and longevity. Finally, let us take the seventh step, and be true companions and remain lifelong partners by this wedlock."

The Hindu wedding ritual is extremely complex and is often performed under a bedi, or outdoor shrine. A priest, on behalf of the bride and groom, makes prayers and offerings, followed by ceremonial rituals, including four circlings around a sacred fire and the nuptial pole. Near the end of the ceremony, the priest ties the groom's sash to the bride's veil and the couple exchanges their wedding vows, which include these traditional Hindu phrasings from the ritual of Seven Steps:

"We have taken the Seven Steps. You have become mine forever. Yes, we have become partners. I have become yours. Hereafter, I cannot live without you. Do not live without me. Let us share the joys. We are word and meaning, united. You are thought and I am sound. May the nights be honey-sweet for us; may the mornings be honey-sweet for us; may the earth be honey-sweet for us; may the heavens be honey-sweet for us. May the plants be honey-sweet for us; may the sun be all honey for us; may the cows yield us honey-sweet milk! As the heavens are stable, as the earth is stable, as the mountains are stable, as the whole universe is stable, so may our union be permanently settled."

Carpatho-Russian Orthodox

This is a sect within the Eastern Orthodox Church that allows spoken vows, as opposed to the traditional silent vows taken during most Eastern Orthodox wedding ceremonies. Carpatho-Russian Orthodox marriage ceremonies are quite formal.

"I,_____, take you, _____, as my wedded wife/husband and I promise you love, honor, and respect; to be faithful to you; and not to forsake you until death do us part. So help me God, one in the Holy Trinity, and all the Saints."

Buddhist

Buddhism is the predominant religion of eastern and central Asia, and is represented by many different sects that profess faith in the complex doctrines of Gautoma Buddha. This is an example of a traditional Buddhist marriage homily:

"In the future, happy occasions will come as surely as the morning. Difficult times will come as surely as night. When things go joyously, meditate according to the Buddhist tradition. When things go badly, meditate. Meditation in the manner of the Compassionate Buddha will guide your life. To say the words 'love and compassion' is easy. But to accept that love and compassion are built upon patience and perseverance is not easy."

> In the Phillippines, a silken cord or string of flowers, also called a nuptial tie, is wound around the necks of the bride and groom.

Episcopalian

The Episcopalian Church in the United States is also known as the Protestant Episcopal Church, a body originally associated with the Church of England. The Episcopalian denomination tends to favor traditional worship services and wedding ceremonies. Here are two slightly different options that are appropriate for an Episcopalian wedding:

"In the Name of God, I _____, take you _____, to be my husband/wife, to have and to hold from this day forward, for better, for worse, for richer, for poorer, in sickness and in health, to love and to cherish, until we are parted by death. This is my solemn vow."

24

An alternative Episcopalian vow is:

"I,_____, take thee, _____, to be my wedded husband/wife, to have and to hold from this day forward, for better, for worse, for richer, for poorer, in sickness and in health, to love and to cherish, till death do us part, according to God's holy ordinance; and thereto I plight/give thee my troth."

American Lutheran

The Lutheran Church was founded by Martin Luther during the Reformation of the 16th century. There are many types of Lutheran churches in America, some favoring traditional worship services, whereas others prefer a more contemporary style. However, all the various synods adhere to the religious teachings of Martin Luther. This is one traditionally accepted wedding vow:

"I take you, _____, to be my husband/wife from this day forward, to join with you and share all that is to come, and I promise to be faithful to you until death parts us."

Presbyterian

Although there are many types of Presbyterian churches, they all generally adhere to the religious doctrines of John Calvin, a 16th-century French theologian and religious reformer. As is true in the Lutheran church, Presbyterian churches vary greatly in their style of worship. In the case of a formal Presbyterian wedding ceremony, however, this is an example of an acceptable vow phrasing:

"I, _____, take you to be my wedded wife/husband, and I do promise and covenant, before God and these witnesses, to be

your loving and faithful wife/husband, in plenty and in want, in joy and in sorrow, in sickness and in health, as long as we both shall live."

Methodist

The Methodist Church in America is a Protestant, Christian denomination with theologies developed from the teachings of John and Charles Wesley. Their worship services, as well as their marriage ceremonies, vary greatly as to their degree of formality. Here is one traditionally accepted wedding vow:

"In the Name of God, I, _____, take you, _____, to be my husband/wife, to have and to hold from this day forward, for better, for worse, for richer, for poorer, in sickness and in health, to love and to cherish, until we are parted by death. This is my solemn vow."

United Church of Christ

The United Church of Christ is a fairly new denomination in America, founded in 1957 by a merger between the Congregational Christian Church and the Evangelical and Reformed Church. In the present Book of Worship, published in 1986, their denomination's preferred wedding vows are stated, reflecting the important concept of giving one's self, as different from taking another. The United Church of Christ vows are:

"_____, I give myself to you to be your wife/husband. I promise to love and sustain you in the covenant of marriage, from this day forward, in sickness and in health, in plenty and in want, in joy and in sorrow, as long as we both shall live."

Unitarian

The Unitarian Church does not offer a standard service, but leaves the composition of the service to each of its ministers. Here are two examples, however, of typical Unitarian-Universalist wedding vows:

The minister asks the bride and groom: "_____, *will you take* _____ *to be your husband/wife; love, honor and cherish him/her now and forevermore?*"

The bride and groom answer: "*I will.*"

Then the minister asks the bride and groom to repeat these words: "*I,*_____, *take you,* _____, *to be my husband/wife; to have and to hold from this day forward, for better or for worse, for richer or for poorer, in sickness and in health, to love and cherish always.*"

The minister asks the bride and groom: "_____, *will you have* _____*to be your husband/wife, to live together in creating an abiding marriage? Will you love, honor, comfort, and cherish him/her in sickness and in health, in sorrow and in joy, from this day forward?*"

The bride and groom answer: "*I will.*"

Quaker

A Quaker wedding is very simple, in keeping with the Quaker tradition. The marriage usually takes place during a regular worship meeting where all in attendance meditate silently while the bride and groom enter and join those already seated. Then, after the traditional Quaker silence, the bride and groom rise, join hands, face each other, and repeat these vows:

"In the presence of God and these our Friends I take thee to be my wife/husband, promising with Divine assistance to be unto thee a loving and faithful wife/husband so long as we both shall live."

The groom speaks his promises first; the bride follows. The bride is not given away, nor does a third person pronounce them married, for the Friends believe that only God can create such a union.

Nondenominational Protestant

There are hundreds of Protestant churches in America that are not affiliated with any particular denomination. Their styles of worship vary, as do their names. For example, you may see nondenominational churches with names such as "Valley Community Church" or "The Little Church in the Vale." Here are several examples of marriage vow phrasings commonly used by this type of church:

"Will you have this woman to be your lawfully wedded wife, to live together in holy matrimony? Will you love her, comfort her, honor and keep her, in sickness and in health, in sorrow and in joy, and forsaking all others, be faithful to her as long as you both shall live?"

A very simple form of the traditional Protestant vow is in the form of a statement made by the minister:

"This celebration is the outward token of a sacred and inward union of the hearts which the Church does bless and the State makes legal...a union created by loving purpose and kept by

abiding will. Is it in this spirit and for this purpose that you have come here to be joined together?"

The bride and groom simply respond: *"Yes, I have."*

The couple joins right hands and recites these traditional vows to each other, either from memory, or by prompting from the officiant:

"I take you to be my wedded wife/husband,

To have and to hold, from this day forward,

For better, for worse, for richer, for poorer,

In sickness and in health, to love and to cherish,

Till death do us part.

This is my solemn vow

According to God's holy ordinance;

And thereto I plight you my troth."

> In ancient China, red was considered the color of love and joy. It was also the color the bride's gown, the ceremony candles, and the rosebud worn by the groom.

"I, _____, take thee, _____, to be my wedded husband/wife, to have and to hold, from this day forward, for better, for worse, for richer, for poorer, in sickness and in health, to love and to cherish, till death us do part, according to God's holy ordinance; and thereto I pledge thee my faith."

Minister (to the groom): *"Wilt thou have _____ to be thy wedded wife, to live together after God's ordinance, in the holy estate of matrimony? Wilt thou love her, comfort her, honor, and keep her, in sickness and in health, and forsaking all others, keep thee only unto her, so long as ye both shall live?"*

Groom: *"I will."*

Minister (to the bride): *"Wilt thou have _____ to be thy wedded husband, to live together after God's ordinance, in the holy estate of matrimony? Wilt thou obey him, and serve him, love, honor and keep him, in sickness and in health, and forsaking all others, keep thee only unto him, so long as ye both shall live?"*

Bride: *"I will."*

❖ ❖ ❖

Groom: *"I _____, take thee _____, to be my wedded wife; and I do promise and covenant, before God and these witnesses, to be thy loving and faithful husband, in plenty and in want, in joy and in sorrow, in sickness and in health, as long as we both shall live."*

Bride: *"I _____, take thee_____, to be my wedded husband; and I do promise and covenant, before God and these witnesses, to be thy loving and faithful wife, in plenty and in want, in joy and in sorrow, in sickness and in health, as long as we both shall live."*

During a Hindu ceremony, a gold ornament, known as a "thali," is tied around the bride's neck. She wears the thali throughout her marriage.

❖ ❖ ❖

Minister (to the groom): "_____, *will you take* _____ *to be your wedded wife, to live together after God's ordinance in the holy relationship of marriage? Will you love her, comfort her, honor and cherish her in sickness and in health, be true and loyal to her, as long as you both shall live?"*

Groom: *"I will."*

Minister (to the bride): "_____, *will you take* _____ *to be your wedded husband, to live together after God's ordinance in the holy relationship of marriage? Will you love, honor and cherish him in sickness and in health, be true and loyal to him, as long as you both shall live?"*

Bride: *"I will."*

❖ ❖ ❖

The bride and groom join right hands, face each other and repeat the vows after the minister.

Groom: *"I,*_____*, take you,* _____*, to be my wedded wife, to live together in God's ordinance in the holy relationship of marriage. I promise to love and comfort you, honor and keep you, in plenty and in want, in joy and in sorrow, in sickness and in health, and forsaking all others, I will be yours alone as long as we both shall live."*

Bride: *"I* _____*, take you,* _____*, to be my wedded husband, to live together in God's ordinance in the holy relationship of marriage. I promise to love and obey you, honor and keep you, in plenty and in want, in joy and in sorrow, in sickness and in health, and forsaking all others, I will be yours alone as long as we both shall live."*

❖❖❖

The bride and groom join right hands, face each other and repeat the vows after the minister.

Groom: "_____, I now take you to be my wedded wife, to live together after God's ordinance in the holy relationship of marriage. I promise to love and comfort you, honor and keep you, and forsaking all others, I will be yours alone as long as we both shall live."

Bride: "_____, I now take you to be my wedded husband, to live together after God's ordinance in the holy relationship of marriage. I promise to love you and obey you, honor and keep you, and forsaking all others, I will be yours alone, as long as we both shall live."

> In Orthodox Jewish custom, the bride (escorted by the two mothers carrying lit candles) circles the groom under the canopy before she takes her place at this right.

$\mathscr{C}$HAPTER TWO
NONTRADITIONAL VOWS

The majority of modern brides and grooms reject traditional wedding vows and recite their own personalized vows instead. The younger the couple, in fact, the less likely they are to subscribe to strict religious or cultural rules and practices. This disregard for tradition began, as I mentioned in the Introduction, back in the 1950s and 1960s. It was triggered by a number of factors, including an increased number of secular, mixed religion, and ecumenical marriages (which demanded a change in the traditional wording) and the rise of liberated women in society (who rejected inequality in male and female roles). Hence, we saw fascinating changes in the wording of wedding vows in the 1990s, when the children of the liberated Baby Boomers began to come of age. More couples today are choosing to develop their own marriage vows than ever before. This chapter offers a large selection of these modern and contemporary phrasings.

> *The Spanish groom gives his bride 13 coins (the giving of "modedas" or "arras") to show his ability to support and care for her. Thirteen represents the number of Christ and his apostles. At the wedding ceremony, the bride carries the coins in a purse or handkerchief.*

"_____, we have come here today to celebrate our marriage. A marriage is a commitment between two people and is spoken publicly before witnesses. And so, _____, I commit myself to you today, before this congregation of family and friends, without reservation or embarrassment of any kind as I say: I love you; I need you; I thank God for you; and I promise to be a good and faithful husband/wife to you so long as we both shall love."

"I bring myself to you this day to share my life with you; you can trust my love, for it's real. I promise to be a faithful mate and to unfailingly share and support your hopes, dreams, and goals. I vow to be there for you always. When you fall, I will catch you. When you cry, I will comfort you. When you laugh, I will share your joy. Everything I am and everything I have is yours, from this moment forth and for eternity."

"Come to me softly, my love; speak to me softly and let me hold your love warm against my heart. May we experience the quiet joys of marriage as our precious love grows deeper through each season. I will be there for you always, holding your hand, as we walk together side by side. I give my life to you this day as your loving, devoted husband/wife, and I promise to be faithful and true to you forever, from this day forth, through all the adversities and joys of life, as long as God gives us on this earth."

"_____, you are God's precious gift to me. You are my springtime, my hope, and my joy. You are everything that's good, pure, and true, and I worship you with my mind, body, and soul. How blessed I am to be able to say that you are mine, to be able to love and cherish you for the rest of my days. I vow to be a good husband/wife to you, _____, always putting you first in my life, always there to comfort you in your sorrow, and rejoice with you in your victories. May our hearts and breath become one as we unite this day as husband and wife. I promise to be your true love from this day forward."

❖ ❖ ❖

"_____, since you came into my life, my days have been bright and glorious, but today, our wedding day, is the brightest of them all, a golden moment, made splendid by our love for each other. And yet, this beautiful moment is only a taste of what is to come as we share our lives together as husband and wife. I pledge my love to you from this day forward. I promise to be faithful and true to you, rejoicing in my good fortune to have found you as my mate."

❖ ❖ ❖

"_____, I searched for you all my life, looking for you, watching for you, needing you, wanting you, but I didn't know who you were until God finally brought you to me, and your love touched my heart. _____, you alone are the love of my life, my dream come true. Now that I've found you, I feel that I've known you always, my soul mate, my precious bride/groom. I was only half a person until you came into my life, but now I am whole and complete. How I love and adore you, _____, and I give myself to you this day with complete joy and abandonment. I promise to be a true and faithful husband/wife, to comfort you, honor you, respect you, and cherish you for all our days together on this earth."

"_____, this is the most significant moment in my life, the moment I give myself to you as your husband/wife, to join with you in holy matrimony. It is such a miracle to have found you, _____. You have made me completely happy because of my deep assurance of your love for me. There is no question of our devout commitment to each other, and I promise to love and cherish you forever as your husband/wife. May this day be just the beginning of an unending joy because of the power of our love."

"The sun smiles on us today, our wedding day, and how can it not? For our love is stronger than forever and our hearts beat together as one. My joy is indescribable as I take you as my husband/wife this day and promise to be a true and faithful husband/wife from this day forward, in all life's circumstances, as we face them together. In the joys and sorrows, the good times and bad, in sickness or in health, I will always be there for you, to comfort you, love you, honor and cherish you, now and forever."

"_____, I vow to be your faithful husband/wife. I offer you my pure and true love and my unwavering support throughout all our lives. As I stand here now, and in the presence of God and these witnesses, I commit myself to you. As we grow and share together, I shall encourage you and strive to help you achieve your full potential as God's creation, then I will celebrate your progress. I give myself to you as I am and as I will be, for all of my life."

"I acknowledge my love for you and invite you to share my life as I hope to share yours. I promise to walk by your side, to love, help, and encourage you. I vow to take time to share with you, to listen and to care. I will share all your laughter and all your tears as your partner, lover, and friend. I promise always to respect you and honor you as an individual and to be conscious of your needs. I shall seek through kindness and compassion to achieve with you the life we have planned together."

"Until I met you, marriage-type love was an abstract thing I only read about in poems, heard sung in romantic love songs, or read about in books. But when I met you I knew for the first time what it was to experience this type of love within my heart. You have made me a believer in the real thing, in the promise of a love that will last a lifetime. There is nothing more important to me in my life than your love. I value it above money, power, or position. I rejoice in our love, and I promise to walk by your side with a constancy that only comes from unreserved commitment, and it is this commitment I make to you now as I take you as my husband/wife, from this day forward and so long as we both shall live."

"_____, I give myself to you on this, our wedding day, and I promise to be a faithful husband/wife, not only for today, as we celebrate our marriage in this beautiful sanctuary, but as an ongoing commitment, through all the ups and downs of life. I do not expect you to fulfill all my dreams, just as I cannot *fulfill all of yours. But I do ask that you share your dreams with me so that I may be your helpmate throughout all the years of our lives. This is my promise."*

❖ ❖ ❖

"It took me a long time to finally find someone I wanted to marry. In fact, my friends used to tease me and say that my goals were too high. But they were met when I found you. I searched for you all my life and, thanks to God, finally found you. You have all the qualities I was hoping to find: You're not only a beautiful person on the outside, but on the inside as well. You're honest, unselfish, loving, caring, supportive, and my ideal woman/man in every way. I have new goals now: to be the faithful, committed husband/wife you deserve. I promise to honor you, respect you, love you, and cherish you as my husband/wife, from this day forward, until the end of time."

❖ ❖ ❖

> *After a Chinese wedding ceremony, the groom's parents host a tea service where the bride and groom pay tribute to their families. First they bow to heaven, then to their heart, and then to their ancestors. Then the couple serves tea to both their parents.*

Bride: "_____, my love for you is eternal."

Groom: "_____, and my love for you is eternal."

Bride: "I give myself to you today as your wife."

Groom: "I give myself to you today as your husband."

Bride: "I promise to love you, honor you, cherish you, and respect you, for all the days of our lives."

38

Groom: *"I promise to love you, cherish you, provide for you, and comfort you, for all the days of our lives."*

Bride: *"We will share our burdens with each other, and so they will seem lighter."*

Groom: *"We will share our joys together, and so they will be multiplied tenfold."*

Bride: *"I thank God for you, my precious groom."*

Groom: *"And I thank God for you, my cherished bride."*

Bride: *"From this day forward I will be faithful to you and always try to be worthy of your love."*

Groom: *"And I will be faithful to you, also trying to be worthy of your love, from this day forward, so help me God."*

Bride: *"So help me God."*

"_____, you light up my life. Before I met you, my days were gray and murky, but your love has changed everything. Every day is a superbly happy adventure since I fell in love with you. The rain is softer, the flowers lovelier, and a child's laughter more joyous, all because of your love. Thank you for loving me and for lighting up my life. I am humbled by your love and thankful to be able to return your love from a heart that is spilling over with joy. This is the happiest day of my life as I take you as my husband/wife and commit myself to you for the rest of our lives."

"I take you, _____, this day as my husband/wife, and I promise to walk by your side forever, as your best friend, your lover, and your soul mate. You are my beloved and I am proud to marry you. I promise to support your dreams and to be there for you for all our lives."

"Every experience we have ever had, everything we have ever done, everything we have ever learned, has brought us to this moment when we stand before these witnesses to take each other as husband and wife. As we confront the future together, I promise to stand by your side, as we face new experiences as man and wife, always growing together, honoring, respecting, and cherishing each other through all life has in store for us. We bring our individual strengths and weaknesses to this marriage, but as we stand together as a married couple, may we complement each other and be exactly what we each need as our love and commitment continue to deepen throughout our married life."

"You have filled my world with meaning. You have made me stronger and more fulfilled as a person. You have made me so happy, and my heart rejoices in the anticipation of spending the rest of my life with you. Thank you for taking me as I am, loving me and welcoming me into your heart. I don't deserve such love, but I'm eternally grateful. I stand here today before these witnesses and take you as my wife/husband. I promise to return your love in full, as we grow

An Irish bride will sew a piece of fine Irish lace into the hem of her wedding gown. She might also carry a fine lace handkerchief.

together as man and wife. I promise to always love you, to be faithful to you, and to cherish and respect you, in all the circumstances that may come to us in our married life."

"I come to you today just as I am, and I take you just as you are, my cherished husband/wife. Let's never change, but always love each other the way we do today, the man and woman we are as we stand here before these witnesses and commit ourselves to each other for life."

Bride: "I give you my hand in marriage."

Groom: "And I give you mine."

Bride: "Take my hand as a symbol of my love."

Groom: "Take my hand as a symbol of my love."

Bride: "I promise to, hold, cherish, and respect you always."

Groom: "I promise to care for you, and to be your friend."

Bride: "As I hold your hand in mine, I feel your love."

Groom: "And I feel your love in my heart. Our love is not only for this moment, but for a lifetime."

Bride: "Yes, for a lifetime."

Up close and personal

I'm a great believer in love at first sight, especially after six years of interviewing engaged couples and helping them plan their weddings! This is one of those heart-tugging stories: Bill and Kathy met in San Francisco when he was a pharmacy student and she was marketing director for a retail clothing store. Their mutual friend, Mike, had just become engaged, and they were both invited to his engagement party. Bill spotted Kathy across the room and immediately asked Mike, "Who is that?" When they were introduced, Kathy's first thoughts were: "Wow! What a great guy! He's cute, outgoing, and potentially successful. Too bad he lives in Colorado."

> The American bride traditionally wears "something old, something new, something borrowed, and something blue." This custom stems from an Old English rhyme.

They were thrown together at a few more social gatherings over that weekend, and as things progressed they each realized there was a spark between them. When the weekend was over, Bill asked Kathy if she would be his official date when he flew back from Colorado for the wedding the following month. Kathy accepted without hesitation, and they spent the next four weeks getting to know each other via lengthy telephone conversations.

By the time they met again a month later at Mike's wedding, they both knew there was something special between them. At the wedding, everyone else sensed this as well and even teased them about the "next wedding." It was so obvious, in fact, that when it came time for Mike to toss the garter, he didn't even bother. He just walked over and handed it to Bill!

Kathy rescheduled her business trips over the next four months so that all her flights "just happened" to connect through Denver, allowing them several weekends to get to know each other. A storybook romance unfolded, and they became engaged one evening when Bill flew to San Francisco to see her. He took her to her favorite restaurant, and then they went for a walk in the moonlight by the Golden Gate Bridge. On bended knee, Mike asked Kathy to marry him, as he slipped a ring onto her finger. She was so overjoyed that she didn't even look at it. Bill asked her, "Aren't you even going to look at your ring?" When she glanced down, she saw that it was a "mood" ring and she didn't know what to think. Bill thought it was hilarious, but finally reached into his pocket for the real thing: a one-carat diamond solitaire. They were married in Colorado the following June in a huge white tent. Everything about their wedding was "picture perfect" until it started to rain and hail, soaking the tent. But it all had a happy ending. Here are their personalized vows:

Minister: *"William and Kathryn stand before us today to declare their promises openly and gladly. William, will you take Kathryn to be your wedded wife? Will you give yourself to her? Will you share completely with her in your life together? Will you promise to be open and honest in your relationship? Will you give her all comfort and support and strength?"*

Bill: *"I will."*

Minister: *"Kathryn, will you take William to be your wedded husband? Will you give yourself to him completely? Will you share completely with him in your life together? Will you promise to be open and honest in your relationship? Will you give him all comfort and support and strength?"*

Kathy: *"I will."*

Minister: *"Kathryn and William, will you now turn and face one another and join hands as you pledge your love and devotion to each other as husband and wife? William, repeat after me:"*

Bill (repeating after the minister): *"I, William, take you, Kathryn, to be my wife; I promise in the midst of our families and friends and in the presence of God to stand beside and love you always; in times of celebration and times of sadness; in times of pleasure and in times of pain; in times of sickness and times of health; I will be with you and love you as long as we both shall live."*

Minister: *"Kathryn, now repeat after me:"*

Kathy (repeating after the minister): *"I, Kathryn, take you, William, to be my husband; I promise in the midst of our families and friends and in the presence of God to stand beside and love you always; in times of celebration and times of sadness; in times of pleasure and in times of pain; in times of sickness and times of health; I will be with you and love you as long as we both shall live."*

> *It is a Filipino wedding tradition to serve roasted pig at the reception, because the pig is considered to be a symbol of fertility and prosperity.*

Bill and Kathy honeymooned for two weeks in Florida and the Grand Cayman Islands. They now live in northern Colorado with their two beautiful daughters, Megan Jean and Molly Anne.

"_____, as you know, it is difficult for me to express my feelings in front of others, especially my very private feelings for

you. But today, as we stand in the presence of our family and friends, I want to publicly declare my love for you. Why do I love you so much? I love you because you are the finest person I have ever known. You are unselfish, loving, gentle, loyal, tender, trustworthy, sympathetic, and a joy to be with. Your laughter, your smile, and your unfailing optimism buoy me, lift me up, and make me a better person. How can I be so blessed as to be loved by you? What could I have ever done in my lifetime to deserve such a treasure? It is a great mystery. My heart overflows with my love for you, and I give myself to you unreservedly today as your faithful husband/wife. I promise to treasure you always, just as I do at this moment."

"I want you for my husband/wife, to be melded into one as we share our lives together. I want to share my joys with you, as well as my sorrows, my hopes, and my dreams. I promise to walk beside you, to support you, care for you, respect you, and cherish you always. You will be the first in my life, my most beloved possession. I promise to be faithful to you no matter what the circumstances of life may bring us. I am proud to become your husband/wife."

"Today, our wedding day, is one brief day in time, and although our vows are spoken in a matter of minutes, they are promises that will last a lifetime. When we leave this ceremony today, I will be a better person, because of you. Because of your love and trust, my life is fulfilled and has a new beginning. I promise to be a faithful husband/wife and worthy of this love. I will be true and loyal to you in every way, always comforting you, loving you, and cherishing you, from this day forward."

Bride: *"Today is a new beginning."*

Groom: *"Yes, we leave our pasts behind and begin a new day."*

Bride: *"We will be partners."*

Groom: *"And we will be friends."*

Bride: *"We will comfort each other."*

Groom: *"We will honor each other."*

Bride: *"We will encourage each other."*

Groom: *"We will uphold each other."*

Bride: *"I vow to be a good and faithful wife."*

Groom: *"And I vow to be a good and faithful husband."*

Bride: *"I want to bear your children, my treasured love."*

Groom: *"And I want to give them to you, my cherished one."*

Bride: *"From this day forward, our life is new."*

Groom: *"Yes, our life is new because of our love."*

"_____, it takes a great amount of trust to pledge one-self to another person for a lifetime. I do that now as I affirm you as my soul mate, my life partner. I will be your dearest friend, your lover, and the father/mother of your children. I accept you, _____, as my husband/wife, and I pledge myself to you without reservation."

Bride: *"I promise, before our family and friends, to be your true, faithful, and loving wife."*

Groom: *"And I promise, before our family and friends, to be your true, faithful, and loving husband."*

Bride: *"I will do everything in my power to keep our love as fresh and strong as it is today."*

Groom: *"And I will be true to you, with my body and my mind, always putting you first in my life."*

Bride: *"Your love has changed my life, and I'm a better person because of you."*

Groom: *"Your faith in me has given me a new confidence and an unexplainable joy."*

Bride: *"I thank God for you and I will love you always."*

Groom: *"And I will love you always. This is my pledge."*

"_____, what a great and beautiful mystery it is for two human souls to join together in marriage, as I do now join with you. I vow to be a faithful, loving husband/wife, to minister to you in sorrow, to share with you in gladness, and to be one with you in the silent joining of our hearts. I pledge myself to you as your best friend. I promise myself to you as your partner. I promise to love you, honor you, comfort you, and cherish you, in sickness and in health, in sorrow and in joy, from this day forward."

Bride: *"Today is our wedding day."*

Groom: *"Yes, today is a sacred day, always to be remembered."*

Bride: *"I come gladly to this moment."*

Groom: *"And I, too."*

Bride: *"From this day forward, our lives will be intertwined as one."*

Groom: *"We will be one flesh."*

Bride: *"I commit myself to you this day, as your faithful and loving wife."*

Groom: *"I commit myself to you this day, as your faithful and loving husband."*

Bride: *"I will nurture you when you need care."*

Groom: *"I will praise you as you succeed in life."*

Bride: *"I promise to share my dreams and my fears."*

Groom: *"I promise to share my hurts and disappointments."*

Bride: *"I promise to soothe your hurts."*

Groom: *"And I promise to calm your fears."*

Bride: *"I promise to be honest with you, never holding back."*

Groom: *"And I promise to put your needs above mine."*

Bride: *"I promise to be the best person I can be, so that our life together will be all it should be."*

Groom: *"And I promise to do everything I can to make you truly happy for the rest of our lives."*

"_____, you are my first love and my last love. Until I met you I didn't give true love much thought. But since you came into my life, I have struggled to find the words to tell you how much I love you. It is difficult for me to verbalize my feelings for you, because mere words can't begin to express my deep love. I thank God for you, _____, and I pledge myself to you now, to be your ever faithful husband/wife. I give you my body, my mind, and my heart, and I promise to love you and cherish you for as long as we both shall live."

Bride: *"This is our wedding day."*

Groom: *"The day we have looked forward to for so long."*

Bride: *"I come to you this day, desiring to be your wife."*

Groom: *"I come to you this day, desiring to be your husband."*

Bride: *"Because of our love, we will be blessed with the joys and comforts of marriage."*

Groom: *"Because of our love, we will endure all trials and cares."*

Bride: *"I will respect and honor you."*

Groom: *"I will cherish and protect you."*

A rice cake is placed on the heads of a Tibetan bride and groom, thus conveying life, health, and wealth to the happy couple.

Bride: *"I will be a tender and affectionate wife."*

Groom: *"I will be a patient and understanding husband."*

Bride: *"As God is my witness, I commit myself to you for all the days of our lives."*

Groom: *"As God is my witness, I commit myself to you for all the days of our lives."*

Bride: *"From this day forward and forever."*

Groom: *"From this day forward and forever."*

"_____, *I love you and I want to be your husband/wife. I promise to be a patient husband/wife, and to always be honest and compassionate. I will be your best friend, your sweetheart, your helpmate throughout life, always putting you first above my own needs. And I promise to live a life that will honor the vows we have spoken. I promise to make you glad to have married me this day."*

"_____, *I take you as my loved husband/wife. You are my miracle. May our lives intermingle, and may our love grow as we become one. You are all I could ever need in my life. You are my friend, my lover, my everything. I promise to be faithful to you, to love you, honor you, live with you, and cherish you, according to the commandments of God, in the holy bond of marriage."*

Groom: "*I love you* _____, *and I promise to be a loving and caring husband. I promise to always cherish your presence and place our marriage above all else.*"

Bride: "*I love you* _____, *and I promise to always be there for you. I promise to receive your love with love and to work hard at keeping our marriage true and everlasting.*"

❖❖❖

"*You are my love, my life, my very breath. Until you came to me, I was searching for you, longing for you. Today we become one flesh as we unite in holy matrimony, a sacred commitment to share our lives together and to be true to each other as long as we both shall live. I promise to give you the best of myself, to respect you as your own person. I promise to bring joy, strength, and imagination to our relationship. I will be your true and faithful husband/wife. This is my solemn vow to you this day,* _____, *so help me God.*"

❖❖❖

"_____, *we have chosen each other as life partners, and today is our wedding day. As we enter this new world of marital bliss, I promise to share all that I am and all that I have. Not just my home and my material possessions, but my inner world, my feelings, concerns, values, joys, hopes, and dreams. I also promise to share your hurts, tears, and failures, as if they were my very own. I will bond to you in love, devote myself to you, and strive to make you happy for all the days of my life.*"

❖❖❖

"_____, today I choose you to be my life partner, and I do so proudly and openly in the presence of these witnesses. I promise to love you always, to listen to you, to nourish you with my praise, to never take you for granted, to hold you close when you need to be held, to laugh with you when you laugh, and to always be your safe haven in this life. I will be faithful to you, even as we grow old together and our bodies age, even when we face illness, and even if we should have financial problems. I will love you truly and joyfully from this moment on. I promise this from my heart, with my soul, and until death parts us."

"Today, I choose you, _____, to be my lifelong partner. I promise to sleep by your side, to be the joy of your heart, the food to your soul, and the best person I can be for you. I promise to laugh with you when times are good, and to suffer with you when they are bad. I promise to wash away your tears with my kisses, and to hold you sweetly and gladly until our days on this earth are over."

"I take you, _____, as my adored and cherished husband/ wife. And I promise to be a loving and faithful husband/wife. May our sunshine be shared, our rains be gentle, and our sweet love eternal. I pledge myself to you from this day forward and for all eternity."

> In a Jewish ceremony, the rabbi will always ask the bride to state her free consent to the union before signing the marriage contract.

"_____, I consider it an honor and a privilege to be the one you have chosen as your life's mate. I promise to be a true and faithful husband/wife, to love you, respect you, and be honest with you always. I promise to be supportive of your goals. As you grow intellectually, emotionally, and spiritually, I will be by your side. Never be afraid to confide in me, because I promise to be a good listener and a safe confidant. You are always welcome into my innermost world, and I promise to share my goals and ideas with you. As we grow together throughout our marriage, there are no limitations on the possibilities of our relationship, and I hope we realize our greatest potential together. I believe in you, _____, and I will be there for you always."

❖ ❖ ❖

"I, _____, in the name of God, take you, _____, to be my husband/wife, from this time onward, to join with you and to share with you all that is to come, to give and to receive, to speak and to listen, to inspire and to respond, and in all our life together to be loyal and to cherish you with my whole being, as long as we both shall live."

❖ ❖ ❖

"_____, I want you to be my husband/wife, not only for the good days, when it's warm and sunny, but for the dark days as well, when it's cold and rainy. May we survive every season and every storm. I want you to live with me. I want to share your thoughts, your hopes, and your dreams. I want you to be my lover, my friend, the mother/father of my children, the heart of our home, and I will stand by your side for all the days of my life. I love you _____."

❖ ❖ ❖

"I, _____, take you, _____, to be my husband/wife, and I commit myself to you. I promise to be responsible in our marriage relationship and to give myself to you in every way. I invite you fully into my being so that I may know who you are, the better to cherish you above all things, and to respect your individuality by always encouraging you to be yourself. I promise to be faithful to you as long as we both shall live."

❖ ❖ ❖

"_____, my beloved, I offer myself to you today as your husband/wife. I offer everything I am, everything I have, and everything I hope to be. I present to you everything that is broken in me, for your touch, your mending, your healing balm of love. It is my desire to be your healer and nurturer. I entrust myself to your heart on this, our sacred wedding day, and for tomorrow, and for all the days of our lives."

❖ ❖ ❖

"_____, you are a kind and gentle man/woman, and it is with great joy that I take you as my husband/wife. May our love grow deeper every day of our marriage, and as the days grow to weeks, and the weeks to months, and the months to years, may we never forget this joyous day and the vows of commitment we are pledging to each other. I will cherish you and be faithful to you for all eternity."

It is tradition for the mother of a Polish bride to give her daughter bread, salt, and wine after she is married, so that she will never lack the necessities of life.

"_____, I take you this day as my cherished wife/husband. You are all I ever dreamed of, or dared to hope for. Only God could have given me such a gift. I choose to marry you this day, and I want to grow old with you. You are the joy of my life, the love of my heart, and my reason for living. I promise to love you forever, as your friend, your lover, and your partner in this world. I commit myself to you for all eternity."

Vows for childhood sweethearts

"_____, we have known each other since childhood when we played together in my backyard, making pancakes in the sandbox, and swinging each other high on the rope swing that Dad hung in the apple tree. We were in preschool together at Mrs. Meredith's, and elementary school, too. Then, in junior high school and high school, we spent many hours together as we studied for exams and attended the games and the school dances. When was it we fell in love? When we were 18? Or 16? Or, maybe when we were 10. For it seems that I have always been in love with you, and I've always wanted you to be my husband/wife. And now, today, we stand here, in the presence of our family and friends, and commit ourselves to each other, to be faithful and true to each other for the rest of our lives. I love you, _____, and I am so thankful we met at such a young age and that our friendship grew into a deep love. I commit myself to you this day, _____, and I promise to be your faithful husband/wife, to love and cherish you, in sickness or in health, in good times or bad, for richer or poorer, from this day forward."

"Remember when we were children and we used to dress up and pretend we were bride and groom? Those were days of playful childish fantasies. But today is for keeps. Today you are a real bride/groom, and I am a real groom/bride. There is no more childishness, no more games of pretend. Today, as I give myself to you as your husband/wife, my mind is clear and my commitment is strong. I am without reservation as I take you to be my life's partner. I will never leave you nor forsake you. I will spend all my days at your side, and leaving behind childish things, we will share a lifetime of eternal, immeasurable love."

"Today is the most important day of our lives, the day we put our individual pasts behind us and go forward into the future as one. We have thousands of memories of our past: our childhoods, the day we met, and the day we knew we were meant to be. But today is the first day of the rest of our lives. From now on we will build new memories together. There will be no more you, and no more me, but only us, from this moment on. I promise to try to be the best husband/wife I can be, so that our memories will be treasures for all the years to come."

> A young bride in Kenya or Nigeria often braids her hair for her wedding day, forming the braids into a crownlike adornment on top of her head.

CHAPTER THREE

VOWS FOR SECOND MARRIAGES

There is always a great deal of heartache when a first marriage dissolves, whether by death or divorce. The estranged man or woman is usually convinced he or she will never be the same again. However, as the popular phrase suggests, time heals all wounds. Over time, the individual might find a new special person with whom to share his or her life.

Second marriages can be just as special as the first, if not more so. This is why most couples feel compelled to write their own personalized vows for a second marriage.

The custom of weaving a circlet of orange blossoms for the bride's head came to America in 1820. Orange blossoms were worn at the White House wedding when Mary Hellen married the son of President John Quincy Adams.

I hope you find the words to express the feelings of your own hearts as you read these poignant, meaningful vows, written by brides and grooms who married for the second time.

"_____, you are my new day, a beautiful ray of light that broke through the darkness of my despair. I thank you for your smile, your sense of humor, and your loving spirit. I promise to love you and cherish you all the days of my life."

❖ ❖ ❖

"_____, you have brought light into the darkness of my life, music to my quiet days, and laughter to my solemn nights. You have revived me and given wings to my heart. Just as the hawk flies high overhead on the wings of the wind, so I will soar on the promise of your love. I give you, from this day forward, the gift of myself, my love, and all that I am. I will fill up the wounds in your heart, just as you will fill mine. In good times or in bad, I will stand by your side and I will die with my love for you still untarnished in my heart."

❖ ❖ ❖

"_____, you are my healer, my comforter, and the joy of my life. Your love has restored my torn, broken heart. Your smile has healed my pain, and your caring spirit has rescued mine from the dark places. I love you, _____, and I vow to be a faithful, loving husband/wife, to care for you, to comfort you, and to cherish you for as long as we both shall live."

> In a Buddhist wedding, the bride and groom are not allowed to display affection towards one another. It is considered disrespectful.

"I, _____, take you, _____, as my lawfully wedded husband/wife. I promise to love you and be true to you in sickness and in health, in good times and bad, always putting you first in my life. I thank the Lord for rescuing me from my despair by sending you to me, my cherished treasure, His most precious and undeserved gift."

"_____, I thank God for you and for the joyous light and peace you have brought to me at a dark time in my life. With a love that will never falter and our abiding faith in one another, I vow to take you, _____, as my husband/wife, to love you, honor you, and cherish you now and forever, so help me God."

"God sent you to me as a precious gift, to heal my broken heart. You have brought sunshine to my soul, joy to my days, and love to my life. I thank God for you, and I take you this day as my husband/wife. May every day of our lives be full of an awareness of our existence for one another. My heart is open and my soul rejoices this day as we become one."

"_____, you are the sunshine of my life after the storms, my sweet nectar after the bitterness of my days, and my joy after the painful seasons of sorrow. I will love you always and forever, my Godsend, my sweet husband/wife, my miracle healer, my lover, my friend. What grace God bestowed when He gave you to me, *and I come to you today joyfully and without reservation, to take you as my lawfully wedded husband/wife, to hold and cherish forevermore. I promise to be faithful to you and to care for you in all circumstances of life, in good times and in bad, in joy and in sorrow, in sickness and in health, so help me God."*

Up close and personal

Kathy, a single mother of two children, was reasonably happy with her life in New Jersey. She says, "I had been divorced for four years, and the last thing I ever wanted was to get remarried. I had made a pretty good life for myself and my children, working as a logistician/secretary for an Army hospital, and although money was really tight, we didn't think we were missing anything. The three of us were very happy. That is, until Joe came along!"

Kathy met Joe, a divorced father, through her children's Boy Scout and Little League activities. They were friends for more than a year before Joe finally asked her on an official "first date." He was being honored at a Boy Scout dinner and asked if she wanted to go with him.

After a year of dating, he proposed in a unique way. They had attended his secretary's wedding and stopped at his home between the ceremony and the reception. Joe asked Kathy to sit down in a swivel chair and close her eyes, which she did. Then he spun her around and told her to open her eyes to see a huge banner on the wall that read, "Kathy, will you marry me?" He was down on his knees by this time and Kathy started to cry. She, of course, said yes.

Although Joe was a construction inspector, he was also a local volunteer fireman, so their wedding had a fireman motif. From the reception to the bride/fireman wedding cake topper to the little fireman helmet place cards, and from their unique wedding invitations to ceremony programs, they incorporated a fireman theme throughout.

Their invitations read this way:

Please join

Kathleen Mary Boyd Welch

and

Joseph Henry McLaughlin

as they take two flames

and

make them one

Friday, the ninth of June

Nineteen hundred and ninety-five

at six o'clock in the evening

Saint James Episcopal Church

Their ceremony programs incorporated fire-related words from the Song of Solomon in the Bible:

Love bursts into flame and burns
Like a raging fire
Water cannot put it out;
No flood can drown it.

61

Kathy says of their vows, "We knew our wedding had to be more personalized than our first ones had been. We knew that the traditional vows were nice, but we needed to say something more personal." They wrote these beautifully worded vows, although the opening was borrowed from a Jewish veil-lifting ceremony:

"O God, who has ordained marriage as the sanctification of the love of man and woman, I turn to Thee in prayer at this solemn moment. I thank Thee for him/her who is about to become my husband/wife and for our love for each other. Enable me to be a worthy wife/husband unto her/him. Grant that our marriage be marked by happiness and mutual devotion.

"Joe/Kathy, these words come from my heart with all my love; with everything I am and everything I have. I love you for what you are to me and what you are to others.

"I will be your husband/wife and your friend, showing pride as both. I will love you when we are together and when we are apart, to stand beside you through life's good times and bad, through sickness and health. I will show compassion when you are sad and joy when you are happy. I will encourage and support all your endeavors. I will give you honesty and sincerity. And I will accept and love your family as my own.

"I give my love, my soul, myself, only to you, starting today, until we are separated by God.

"Joe/Kathy, I give you this ring with all that I have and with all that I am. It represents my love for you. And as that, it shows no beginning and no end. I ask that you wear it as an outward symbol of my love and that it may remind you, and to show others, how much you mean to me."

When Princess Elizabeth of
England married the Duke of
Edinburgh in 1947, their wedding
cake was 9 feet tall and weighed
more than 500 pounds.

❖ ❖ ❖

", your smile is a tonic to my battered soul, a healer
of my broken heart, a blessing beyond description. How thankful
I am to have found you at last, my soul mate, my other half. As we
become one flesh today, I am overwhelmed by my love for you. I
adore you, and I worship you with my body, mind, and spirit. I
pledge to be a good and faithful husband/wife, always tender in
my feelings toward you, always true to you throughout all circumstances of life, from this day on and forever."

❖ ❖ ❖

"As we begin our new life together as husband and wife, I am
amazed at our love. It is an invisible thing, our love, and yet it is a
force so strong that it will hold our lives together for all the years
to come. Our past is over; our future is new, and as we take our
vows today, we will be changed forever, and I take them gladly,
and without reservation. , I commit myself to you, to
be your loving, faithful husband/wife. I promise to honor you,
believe in you, protect you, and do everything in my power to
make your life happy and fulfilled. This is my promise. Take my
hand as we go with joy into our new life together."

❖ ❖ ❖

"_____, when God brought you into my life, everything changed. Because of you, I laugh, I smile, I dare to dream again. All the heartaches and sorrows are behind me now, and by God's grace, and because of you, I look forward, with great joy, to spending the rest of my life with you, my love. I look forward to caring for you, nurturing you, being there for you in all life has for us, and I vow to be a true and faithful husband/wife, for as long as we both shall live, so help me God."

"From your first hello on the day we met, there was fresh meaning to my life. You came to me and you were mine from that first moment, brought to me by God's grace, just in time to rescue me from my empty world. You've filled my heart with your love and as we marry this day, my life is finally complete. I know that for the rest of my days you'll always be there for me, and I for you. My love for you cannot be measured, and I promise to devote the rest of my life to you, as a tender and faithful husband/wife, always putting you first, caring for you, and loving you through all the ups and downs of life from this day forward."

"_____, God has given us a second chance at happiness, and I praise Him for that. I come today to give you my love, to give you my heart and my hope for our future together. I promise to bring you joy, to be at home with your spirit, and to learn to love you more each day, through all the days of our lives. I promise to be your faithful wife/husband. My love for you is seamless, endless, and eternal."

"When I first met you, _____, I was drawn to you immediately, but I was resigned never to marry again, after the pain I
had suffered through the years. But your love was so tender and
genuine, so compassionate and caring, until you crept slowly into
my life. Inch by inch you permeated my being, as your love fell
softly onto my heart. You have turned my life around. Because of
your love, each day is a new delight, a new awakening. My heart
belongs to you, dear _____, and I pledge here today, in the
presence of these witnesses, to be your faithful husband/wife, to
stand beside you, upholding you, cherishing you for the rest of
our lives."

"_____, I am proud to marry you this day and become
your husband/wife. I promise to wipe away your tears with my
laughter, and your pain with my caring and my compassion. We
will wipe out the old canvas of our lives and let God, with His
amazing artistic talent, fill them with new color and beauty. I give
myself to you completely as your husband/wife and I promise to
love you always."

"_____, we are blessed beyond measure this day as we
stand here, bound by our eternal love. How I thank God for bringing you to me, my beloved, as a healer to my soul and as a hope
for my future. I promise to be faithful to you, to honor you, to
grow with you through the years, to suffer with you, to rejoice
with you. Because I have never known such a love as this before,
I take you now and forever as my dear husband/wife."

"*Today I have come to marry my best friend, my life-saver, my sweetheart. Before I met you, I was only half a person, a broken man/woman, filled with sadness and regret. But your love has made me whole again. Together we will face life with gladness and thanksgiving, welcoming all God's blessings in store for us. I am humbled by your love, and I will stay with you, in love, for all of our days. I accept you as my husband/wife; will you accept me as your husband/wife?*"

Up close and personal

I would like to close this chapter by telling you another true story of a couple I know; I'll call them Bill and Anna, to protect their identities. Bill and Anna lived two doors apart in a Northern California suburb when they were growing up, and they played together every day.

By the time Bill and Anna were in junior high school they were sweethearts and never dated anyone else until after their high school graduation. It was then that Bill went away to college and fell in love with, and eventually married, someone else. Soon

> In Costa Rica, the "hoke of matrimony" (a white cord) is looped around the necks of the bride and groom by the priest as a blessing.

after, Anna found someone else. She married him and soon gave birth to a baby boy.

After they had been married for about five years, they were each divorced. Bill's wife left him one day while he was at work. She left a note saying, "Bill, I don't love you anymore. I never loved you. I'm leaving you." Bill was shocked and devastated. Meanwhile, Anna discovered that her handsome husband was a drug addict, which led to heated arguments between them. Their last day together was the day he abused her.

Bill and Anna each moved back home with their families and eventually began seeing each other, first simply as friends trying to comfort each other through the grief. Eventually they realized how much they loved one another and had, in fact, always loved one another.

Bill and Anna were married in a beautiful garden wedding as they stood before the minister with Anna's son between them, each of them holding one of his hands. It was one of the most poignant, emotional, tearful weddings I've ever witnessed. Here are the touching vows they wrote for their wedding:

"Anna, mere words cannot express my love for you, my need for you, my joy in finding you after suffering such heartache and grief. I have been stumbling around this earth, only half a man, with a dark, gaping hole in my heart. But your love has filled that void completely, and I am whole again. As we become one flesh on this our wedding day, I vow to be a loving, faithful husband, always rejoicing in you and praising God for you, until death do us part."

"Bill, God, the healer of broken hearts, has rescued us in His perfect time, and has given us to each other to love and to cherish

for all the days of our lives. I promise to love and honor you, in all faith and tenderness, to live with you according to the ordinance of God, in the holy, sacred bond of marriage."

Don't you just love a happy ending?

> In Ancient Greece, the bride was greeted and joined by friends as she walked from her home to the altar. This became known as the "Bride's Processional."

*C*HAPTER FOUR
Vows that include children

It has become quite natural for the children of the bride or groom to be included in the wedding ceremony, serving as attendants or participants in the service itself.

It is commonly felt that by bringing a child into the wedding experience and helping him or her feel an integral part of it, the easier it will be for him or her to accept a new mommy or daddy and to feel part of the new family being newly created at this ceremony.

In addition to including the children in the wedding ceremony, it's a nice touch to order flowers for the children: a boutonniere for a boy and a small wrist corsage for a girl.

The ancient Greeks made wedding-day offerings to Zeus, who disapproved of marriage. To protect the bride from his displeasure, she was often whisked away at nightfall and seated between the groom and his best friend.

Here are the ways several couples have included their children in their weddings. I think it's a lovely new trend to include children in the ceremony.

Minister: *"And do you, _____, take _____ as your own child, promising to love him/her and care for him/her, providing for his/her needs, both physical and spiritual?"*

Groom/Bride: *"I do."*

Minister (addressing the child): *"And do you, _____, take _____, to be your loving father/mother from this day forward?"*

The child: *"I do."*

Groom/Bride (addressing the child): *"_____, I place this ring on your finger as a sign of my loving promise made this day."*

❖ ❖ ❖

"I love you, _____, and I love your children as my very own. My joy is multiplied tenfold because of _____ and _____. Their love fills a void in my life, a place that has remained empty for all of these years. We are a family, and I am blessed beyond belief as I marry you this day. I vow to be a true and faithful husband/wife to you, in sickness or in health, in joy or in sorrow, in good times or in bad, from this day forward and forever. I don't take my responsibilities as a father/mother lightly, but with great gravity and sincerity. I vow to be a loving, tender, and nurturing father/mother as well, always there for _____ and _____, not only providing their physical needs, but their emotional needs as well. I vow to always be a good listener, a loving counselor, and a faithful friend."

> During the Ch'ing Dynasty, Chinese weddings had puppet shows and musicians. The bride's gown was typically embellished with orchids, pomegranates, and butterflies.

70

"Because of you, my heart is at peace at last. Because of you, I am happy and stable. Because of you, I look forward to the future with joy instead of dread. Because of you, my world is whole again. Because of you, I believe in marriage anew. And because of you, my children will be blessed with a loving mother/ father. You are the kindest, gentlest, most loving person I have ever met. What a blessing that I met you, and that our friendship grew into a love that is eternal. I commit myself to you this day as your husband/wife and as the mother/father of your children. May God bless our marriage and our new family."

Up close and personal

This is a true story that is very dear to my heart, because it is the love story of my son and the woman he married. One summer afternoon, when Darren was playing his trombone with a Sacramento jazz band at a charity concert, he noticed a stunning woman in the audience. He couldn't take his eyes off of her. There was quite a crowd that day, and she slipped away after the concert before he could come up with a way to meet her, although he did ask around to see if anyone knew who she was. Two months later his band was playing for another fund-raiser when he saw her in the audience, and this time he wheedled an introduction. She told Darren immediately about her recent divorce and her young son, expecting Darren to lose interest. He didn't, however, and he convinced her to take his telephone number and give him a call sometime.

After an agonizing week of waiting, Darren finally heard from her, and the two of them hit it off immediately over the phone. After a week of telephone conversations, they agreed to meet at a restaurant for dinner, which became their first date.

Darren and Lisa soon got to know one another, fell in love, and were eventually married. Lisa's son, Jeffrey, was 3 years old at the time of the wedding, and this is the vow Darren wrote and recited to him that day:

"Jeffrey, I promise to be there as a father to you, to protect you, to support and comfort you and our family, and to love you all the days of my life."

I usually do a pretty good job of keeping my emotions under control during a wedding, but this was one time I couldn't stop the tears. In fact, both my husband and I had a tough time controlling our emotions because of the joy we felt for all three of them. We were so happy for Darren to have finally found Lisa, such a beautiful person inside and out. But to also have little Jeffrey as part of our family was almost more joy than our hearts could bear.

"I vow to be a good and faithful husband/wife to you, _____, but I also vow to be a patient, loving father/mother to _____, _____, and _____, caring for them and providing for them as my own. I vow to be their strength and their emotional support, loving them with all my heart from this day forward."

"As we become one on this, our wedding day, we become part of each other: Your feelings become my feelings; your sorrows become my sorrows; your joys become my joys; your worries become my worries, and your children become my children. I promise to be a true and faithful husband/wife and father/

mother, always there to comfort you, rejoice with you, and endure all the complexities of life that we will face together as a
family in the years to come. My love for you and the children is
pure and unshakable and I hereby commit myself to all of you
from this day forth."

In a recent wedding on a yacht, a couple recited their vows. The
bride stood with her two children at her side. When the minister
asked her: *"Do you take this man?"* she turned to her two children, bent down, and spoke with them privately for a moment.
Then she turned back to the minister and said: *"I do."*

When a couple is married in Bavaria,
local tradition says that the bride
should arrive at the church on a hay
cart. After the ceremony, the couple
must saw a log in half.

This small gesture gave
her children a feeling of
being included in her
vows.

"I have promised to
love you and to be a faithful husband/wife, but I would like to
add another vow, a promise to love _____ as my own child,
to provide for him/her and to be a faithful father/mother, always
concerned for his/her welfare and his/her every need."

"_____, did you know that you are a little bit of heaven to
me? Although the golden days of childhood come and go so
quickly, I promise that I will always be there for you. I love you
dearly and I promise to be a faithful father/mother to you for all
the days of my life."

Vow to a new stepdaughter

"_____, I love your mommy, and today I have taken her as my wife. But do you know that I love you dearly as well? I want to be as a father to you, and I invite you into my heart. We will have happy times together, you and your mommy and I. With this ring I give you my love._" (Slides a ring onto the girl's finger. Alternatively, a necklace or other item may be used.)

Vow to a new stepson

"_____, I love your daddy, and today I have taken him as my husband. But do you know that I love you dearly as well? I want to be as a mother to you, and I invite you into my heart. We will have happy times together, you and your daddy and I. With this ring I give you my love._" (Slides a ring onto the boy's finger. Alternatively, a special watch or other item may be used.)

Up close and personal

Ben, a cattle rancher, and Wendi, a pharmacy technician, met at California State University during the fall semester of 1993. They were friends for several months before they started dating. After some time, Wendi's 3-year-old daughter, Cheyenne, began calling Ben "Daddy," completely on her own. When Ben and Wendi were married, following their traditional vows, the minister asked Cheyenne, who served as a flower girl and was standing a few feet away, to come stand beside Ben. Then these words were spoken:

Minister: "_Ben, do you wish to receive Wendi's daughter Cheyenne as your own daughter?_"

Ben: "_I do._"

Minister: *"Do you promise to love her, raise her, guide her, teach her, and be a father to her?"*

Ben: *"I do."*

Minister: *"Do you have something you would like to give her?"*

Ben: *"Yes."*

Ben then took a tiny heart-shaped ring from his pocket, knelt down, and placed the ring on Cheyenne's finger, followed by a hug and a kiss.

At the end, the minister introduced the couple to the congregation as "Mr. and Mrs. King, and daughter, Cheyenne." Ben loves and adores Cheyenne as much as he would if they were biologically related, and Cheyenne tells people that "she's married to Ben." She didn't think it was fair, however, that she couldn't go on the honeymoon!

Family medallion ceremony

The family medallion is a beautiful round medal that has three intertwined circles, symbolizing family,

> *During an Orthodox Jewish wedding service, the bride and groom and their two honor attendants stand under a "chuppah," a canopy made of flowers or cloth.*

love, and unity. The first two circles represent the union of the man and woman, and the third circle represents the children who are intertwined in their love. The medallion is placed on a chain, forming a necklace, which is placed over each child's neck following the couple's wedding vows.

As the parents place the medallions over the necks of their children, they pledge to love and support their children as they become part of their family unit. You can alter these words to fit the structure of your new family, but here is a nice general phrase:

"_____, _____, and _____ *(the first names of the children), today we have become husband and wife, but we have also become a precious new family. I promise to be the best father/mother I can possibly be, as I care for you, protect you, support you, and love you with all my heart for all the days of my life."*

Circle of acceptance ceremony

This is a sweet ceremony that takes place in front of the altar. You, your children, and the officiant stand in a circle and hold hands. This ceremony give the children the opportunity to feel a part of the marriage and the new family that results.

There are many variations to this ceremony. However, the officiant usually addresses each child, saying something similiar to:

Officiant: "_____, *your mommy and your new daddy want you to feel accepted into your new family that is being formed today. They also want your blessing. Do you, _____, accept your new family circle?*

Child: *"Yes."*

> *Many weddings follow the Roman tradition of celebrating in the spring, when homage was originally paid to the three divinities: Cres, Maia, and Flora.*

Family unity candle ceremony

A traditional unity candle ceremony consists of the lighting of a large central candle from two separate candles held by the bride and groom, to symbolize the uniting of two lives into one.

A family unity candle ceremony is similar to the one described, except that there are additional candles, one for each child. The bride, groom, and each child light the central candle at the same time, symbolizing that they have formed a new family unit, unified as one. A variation of this procedure is for the bride and her children to hold one candle, and the groom and his children to hold the other candle. These two candles are used to light the central candle at the same time. Another poignant variation is for the bride and groom to light the central candle from their respective candles, then light their children's candles from the wick of the central candle.

Children included in congregational blessing

Children are often included as part of the congregational blessing upon the bride, groom, and their child or children.

Minister to the congregation: *"Will you lend your hearts and concerns to this couple and their children, upholding them in prayer and encouraging them in their new life together?"*

The congregation responds: *"We will."*

Up close and personal

As I close this chapter, I have one more little story. A friend of mine took a Caribbean cruise recently and witnessed a poolside wedding. The bride and groom evidently brought their families along for the wedding, and the bride's teenage daughter served as her maid of honor. During the ring ceremony, after the groom had recited his ring vows and placed a wedding ring on his bride's finger, he unexpectedly reached inside his pocket and pulled out a delicate gold-banded birthstone ring, which he placed on the finger of the bride's daughter, symbolizing her inclusion in the marriage.

> *On their wedding morning, Hopi couples greet the rising sun, and pray for a good life together, for children, and for faithfulness.*

CHAPTER FIVE
REAFFIRMATION VOWS

A reaffirmation ceremony is a time of thanksgiving for the couple's many years together. It is also a strengthening of their marriage commitment. By the time a couple have been married 10, 25, 40, or even 50 years, they have successfully survived a myriad of crises in their lives through their deep love for each other. The couple's reaffirmation vows may be personalized to reflect this. Alternatively, a couple may prefer to duplicate their original wedding ceremony as closely as possible, including the original minister, if he is still available. The members of the original wedding party are often included, along with the celebrating couple's extended family of children, grandchildren, nieces, and nephews.

During the Timbangan ritual in a Javanese wedding, the couple sits on the lap of the bride's father, who is seated on a special wedding couch. He says that they both weigh the same, meaning that they will be loved equally by both sets of parents.

Many families create exhibits and displays honoring the couple, including photographs taken on their wedding day, the original wedding certificate, a photograph of their first home, family snapshots and scrapbooks, a photo montage of the couple and all their family members, their original wedding album, plus a sentimental item or two unique to their life together. For those couples who would like to personalize their reaffirmation vows, this chapter offers many touching choices. Please adjust the details (for example, how you met, how long you dated, when you married, and so on) to reflect your own relationship.

A very simple way to handle the vows in a reaffirmation ceremony is for the minister to read the actual vows that were made at the couple's wedding ceremony, then ask the couple if they do freely reaffirm those vows right at that moment. The pastor or minister may ask, after reading their original vows: *"Remembering these vows, made so many years ago on _____, do you now reaffirm these vows and your love for each other?"*

The couple answer: *"I do."*

"I thank God, our Father, for bringing us together to love and care for each other. Every year, as we have walked through our days together, whether joyous or difficult, I thanked God to have you by my side. You have always been there for me, _____, filled with love, understanding, and encouragement, freely offering a smile and a hug. Today, as we reaffirm our wedding vows, I commit my life to you anew and I vow to be a loving, true and faithful husband as long as we both shall live."

"_____, ours has been a fairy-tale love story. From that first day we met until this very moment, our love has been one to be envied. We have been partners who grew more and more in love each day as we journeyed through life together. Our children have been the fruit of our love, and our grandchildren as well. We

have a lifetime of shared memories, shared joys, shared sorrows, and our love has soared above it all. Today, as we renew our wedding vows before our beloved friends and family, I do so as an expression of how much I love and adore you. Ours is a love story destined to continue until death do us part."

"As we stand here today renewing our wedding vows, I recall our wedding day so well. We were so young, so hopeful, so full of dreams. And most of our dreams have come true. But not all. And the disappointments hurt more than we thought they would, didn't they? And yet, our good times together were even better than we expected. If I could have known then what I know now, would I have married you? Yes, most certainly, with the same joy and commitment I feel today, as I promise to be your devoted and faithful husband/wife for whatever years we have left in this life."

Up close and personal

Mary was a cheerleader and one of the prettiest girls in the school, and Jim was the quarterback of the football team and popular with everyone on campus. Mary was two years younger than Jim, so he graduated and went off to college ahead of her. Their relationship held, however, as their tender love letters flew back and forth. He drove home to see her on weekends as often as he could. That is, if he could get his old Plymouth up and running.

Mary graduated from high school in June of 1955, and they were married that August. They moved into a married couples' dormitory at Jim's university, and he finally graduated with a degree in psychology that he intended use in a teaching career. After his graduation, however, Jim and Mary's future took an abrupt turn as they accepted a call to become home missionaries on a Native American reservation in Arizona. This decision set the course for the rest of their married lives. Their missionary service was followed eventually by full-time service in the ministry.

Last summer, Jim and Mary's four children planned an elaborate reaffirmation ceremony for their parents' 40th wedding anniversary. Other than the 25th anniversary ceremony of Barbara Mandrell and her husband, which I had watched on television, I had never seen a full-fledged reaffirmation wedding ceremony with all the trimmings. Jim and Mary's service was held in the elegantly decorated sanctuary of the church they pastored, and Mary was given away by her older brother. Their children served as their attendants, their grandsons as ushers, and their young granddaughters as bell ringers (girls who travel up and down the aisles ringing delicate crystal bells to announce the beginning of the ceremony).

Jim and Mary's children, who are gifted singers and musicians, provided the music. Their eldest daughter made a three-tiered wedding cake, complete with Jim and Mary's original bride-and-groom cake topper that had been carefully packed away for 40 years. The minister who had married them in 1955 came out of retirement to conduct the service and wrote these personalized vows that reflected the couple's life of sacrificial service to God and to each other:

> *Tradition says that June is a lucky month for weddings because of its ties with Juno, the Roman goddess of marriage and femininity.*

"When I married you on that August afternoon in 1955, you had no idea what God had in store for you. You served as missionaries under very difficult circumstances, often doing without the

necessities of life as you depended on the love offerings of others for your survival. When you took your wedding vows that day you promised to love each other whether richer or poorer, and you kept that vow as you remained true to each other and true to your Lord through those difficult times. Your unique circumstances required great faith, and your faith never wavered. I know you count all your hardships as sheer joy, however, because of the blessings He has given you: four children who love and respect you, nine adoring grandchildren, and much fruit in your ministry.

"And so, as you come today to reaffirm your wedding vows and as you reflect back over all your years together as husband and wife, do you now reaffirm the vows you took 40 years ago? If so, repeat them after me: "I, Jim/Mary, take you, Mary/Jim to be my husband/wife; to have and to hold from this day forward, for better, for worse, for richer, for poorer, in sickness and in health, to love and to cherish always."''

After their vows were affirmed and it was time for Jim to kiss his bride, he surprised everyone, including her, by presenting her with a diamond suspended on a delicate gold chain. What had everyone in tears was the look of love in Jim's eyes as he fastened the gold chain around Mary's neck and murmured some very quiet and private words of endearment before he kissed her. It was obvious to all that they are still very much in love.

❖ ❖ ❖

"On we took our vows as we stood in this very place. My knees were shaking as I recall, and although I gave my heart to you that day as I recited my vows, I spoke haltingly, feeling some apprehension as we entered the fearful state of matrimony. As I look back now, surveying our years of married life, I have a grateful reminiscence in my heart because of the

blessed fulfillment our marriage has been. I give thanks for our life together, which has been rich beyond measure, and today I reaffirm my wedding vows, but this time with a clearer head and absolute assurance in my heart. There are no hesitations or second thoughts today as I promise with all my heart to love and cherish you for all the blessed days we may yet spend together on this earth."

"You are still my bride, my precious one, as beautiful and lovely as the day I married you. You are the most important person in my life, and I intend to keep it that way. Our marriage has succeeded, while so many have failed, because we have kept the laughter and thrown out the pain. Although we have winked at life and laughed at its transient problems, we have always taken our marriage seriously. Yes, marriage is a fragile thing, and one that has lasted as long as ours is a precious rarity, to be held carefully and cherished forever. As we celebrate our _____ anniversary today, in the presence of these witnesses, I hereby reaffirm my vows, to love you, comfort you, honor and keep you, in sickness and in health, in sorrow and in joy, and to be faithful to you as long as we both shall live."

"My dear _____, you are a revered wife/husband and mother/father, always filling our hearts with your love. You have kept our home peaceful and have been a gracious host/hostess to all who have graced us through the years. Your children rise up and call you blessed, and your friends stand by you, eternally grateful for the love you have extended as you've helped and comforted those in need. You are the most unselfish man/woman I know and I consider it an honor to have been married to you for

_____ years. Today, in the presence of God and this precious company of friends and family, I freely and publicly renew my wedding vows, pledging again my unwavering love as your faithful husband/wife from this day forward. May the Lord bless us with many more happy years together."

❖ ❖ ❖

"I can't believe how lucky I was to find you years ago, and I was luckier still when you agreed to marry me. And hasn't our marriage been good, with so many memories of beautiful moments shared? I truly treasure those memories. They are souvenirs in my heart, memories of you as my best friend, my lover, my husband/wife. Our marriage is the most important thing in my life, and you are the most important person. As our love has grown deeper each year, our relationship has gone far beyond anything I could have imagined. As we stand before this gathering of our friends and family, I publicly and joyfully reaffirm our wedding vows."

A Finnish bride wears a golden crown at the ceremony. During the reception, she is blindfolded and surrounded by the unmarried women. The bride will attempt to crown one of them, and folklore says that the newly crowned woman will be the next one to marry.

❖ ❖ ❖

" years ago, I chose you to be my husband/wife, and today I choose you again. Not because I should, not because it is expected, and not because I have no other choice, but because my love for you is even richer and deeper than the day I married you, and I choose you again gladly and without reservation. Choosing each other is an ongoing process, my love, and every morning, as I look at your precious face, I choose you anew and rejoice in the fact that you have chosen me, too. How blessed I am to have you as my husband/wife. You have met all my expectations and given me a life filled with joy. I want to live with you for the rest of my life, not because I should, or because it is expected, but because that is the longing of my heart."

"I fell in love with you the first time when we were in high school. And throughout our married life, I have fallen in love with you again hundreds of times for a hundred different reasons. We've shared our dreams and built our castles in the air, but when things have been rough and I've been afraid, yours is the hand I want to hold. You are the source of my strength. You are still the only man/woman for me, and when I think of the years that still lie ahead of us, I fall totally and completely in love with you all over again. How I love you at this moment, _____, and I vow to be a good and faithful husband/wife for all the rest of our days."

Husband to his wife: "I remember that Saturday morning, _____ years ago, when you walked down the aisle and into my arms, my beautiful bride. We had such great expectations of each other, didn't we? We hoped that every day would be as glorious and happy. Every day wasn't as glorious and happy as that day, as we discovered through our years together, but you never disappointed me. Your love was constant and steady. You were always

> Tradition calls for a Welsh bride to give her attendants cuttings of myrtle from her bouquet.

there for me, no matter what the circumstances. How I love you still, my beautiful bride, and how proud I am to be your husband. I will gladly renew the promises I made to you _____ years ago, and I pledge myself to you again this day with a love as fresh as the day I married you."

"You are mine, my love, and I am yours, as ordained by God from the beginning of time. He brought us together and He has kept us together, to love and be loved, to cherish and be cherished, for all the days of our lives. You are God's gift to me, my priceless treasure, my blessing for life. May He bless us as we come together today to renew our pledge of love to one another."

"Remember the first time we met? You were dancing with someone else. I cut in on that poor soul, and we have been dancing together ever since. Our life's dance has been a steady dance, weaving in and out of our days and years together. It's been a quiet, intimate dance of shared thoughts and dreams, through many summers of new-mown grass, and through cold, chilling winters. Today we continue our life's dance with a commitment that is as fresh and joyous as the day I married you. Dance with me, _____, until the day I die."

"Do you remember all our years together, _____? There have been _____ of them. There were those first years, when we were so excited about being married and having our babies. Then, there were those difficult years as we struggled to raise teenagers in a dangerous world. Finally, there were those empty-nest years when our children married and went out on their own. But as I reflect back on all our married days, and I picture you the times you sat feeding _____ in the big rocker in the den, and that Halloween you dressed up like Big Bird for _____'s party, and the time in the hospital when you held me close after my accident...all these remembrances fill my heart to overflowing with my love for you. You have been a devoted, loving wife/husband and mother/father and there are no words to express how deep and rich is the love I feel for you this day. I am proud to be your husband/wife and I gladly renew my vows as we celebrate our _____ anniversary."

❖ ❖ ❖

"_____, you have been my all, my life for all these years, a loving devoted mother/father and grandmother/grandfather, always giving of yourself with Christ-like, sacrificial love. You have put our needs and cares above your own, always nourishing and supporting. You are a Godly man/woman, seeking His help in all ways and living His love through your words and deeds. I come to you today, my precious, adored husband/wife and give myself to you afresh and anew, as we renew our wedding vows, first pledged _____ years ago, in this very place. In the presence of our family and friends, I honor you today and I vow to be a faithful husband/wife from this day forward, for as long as the Lord lets us live on this earth."

❖ ❖ ❖

"Thank you, _____, for being such a kind, nurturing, loving husband/wife and father/mother. I am so grateful to have found you at such a young age, and that our friendship grew into a love that committed itself to a lifelong marriage. After _____ years of living with you, loving you, and appreciating you, my love for you has deepened and matured. Today, as we stand before our family to reaffirm our wedding vows, I do so with a heart that is overflowing with my love for you, my cherished husband/wife. I give you every measure of myself, committing myself to you anew, as we look forward to the wonderful, challenging years yet in store for us as a married couple."

Wife to her husband: "When I was a young woman, I had dreams of being married someday, and when you came along, you were truly my knight in shining armor. After _____ years of marriage, I can honestly say, as God is my witness, that you have been all I could have imagined or hoped for: my lover, my companion, my friend, my nurturer, my comforter, my playmate, and a model father. I am so lucky to have found you, and I pray to be worthy of such a man. Today, as we celebrate our anniversary, I gladly and joyfully take you again as my husband and I promise anew, as I vowed on our wedding day, to love and respect you, for richer or poorer, in sickness or in health, for better or worse, until death do us part. Thank you for being my knight in shining armor."

A Jewish couple usually signs an elaborately embellished "ketubah," or marriage contract, which is then hung in a prominent place in the couple's new home.

"_____, thank you for your love and your faithfulness to me all these years. It's easy to love someone at first, when we look our best, say the right thing, and are always on our best behavior. But you have seen me at my absolute worst, and still you love me, which makes me love you all the more. Thank you for always being there for me, in every way, and thank you for all you will be to me in the years to come. I pledge again to you this day to love you for the rest of our days."

"We took our wedding vows 25 years ago, and though many things have changed in our lives since then, one thing has remained constant: our love. We had babies and watched them grow up. We built two homes and sold them. We've moved 8 times. We've owned 12 cars. We've suffered through times of illness and times when the paycheck didn't stretch enough to pay the bills. But through it all, my love for you has remained. In fact, although it seems impossible, I believe I love you more every year we are married. I'm so glad I married you that day 25 years ago, and I gladly renew my wedding vows this day. I promise to love you, honor you, cherish and keep you, for better or worse, for richer or poorer, for all the years of our lives. _____, I want you to know that whatever may face us in the years to come, I will always love you."

"_____, what a good marriage we have had for 25 years! Who would ever believe that after all these years we love each other even more than we did on our wedding day? In fact, our love has been a precious love. You have been everything a wife/husband could ever hope for: a compassionate friend, a caring listener, a patient nurse, an exemplary mother/father, and a truly enthusiastic partner as we have pursued our dreams and goals. Thank you for making me so happy in every way. You are still my sweetheart, and I gladly reaffirm my wedding vows this day."

"50 golden years! How I praise God for you,_____. It was such a stroke of luck to have met you that day, and yet, was it really luck, or God's providence? I loved you from that first time I saw you as you stood there with those glorious auburn curls and those sparkling emerald eyes. Who would have believed you would ever give me a chance? But, you did. And now, 50 years later, I still love you as much as I did the first time I saw you. When we married we promised to be faithful in good times and in bad, whether richer or poorer, in sickness and in health, and we have had our share of all of these, haven't we? But we have been faithful and our love has grown as we have overcome many obstacles during our 50 years of marriage. How can I thank you for the joy you have brought into my life, for your laughter, your hugs and your constant, unshakable love? I recommit myself to you this day, _____, as your husband/wife, and I promise to love you for always, just as I did 50 years ago, and just as I do today."

> Greek-American brides throw a pomegranate, rather than the typical bouquet, during the reception. The pomegranate fruit symbolizes fertility.

Up close and personal

This chapter wouldn't be complete without the story of a golden anniversary couple.

Erma and Loren knew each other all their lives, but fell in love when they were teenagers in the 1940s. They realized their love had turned to marriage-type love, however, during the summer of 1945 when she was 17 and he was 20. It all began one Saturday in June when Erma and her sister, Fern, walked from their home to the Uptown Ballroom in Modesto, California, where Loren asked Erma to dance. A week and a half later Loren showed up at

Erma's home unannounced and asked her out on a date, "right in front of all of my family," as Erma writes. He took her to a fall carnival where he conveniently steered her over to the Fun House, where her pleated skirt just happened to blow over her head as a gust of air suddenly spurted from beneath the floor boards. Quite embarrassed, Erma turned to Loren and asked, "Did you see anything?" With a smile, he said no, but years later he told her it was "just a good thing you were wearing panties!"

They dated nearly every day after that and he proposed a few months later when he told her he loved her and wanted her to be the mother of his children. Their parents weren't keen on them getting married, so Erma and Loren decided to elope. On December 30, 1945, they took off for Carson City, Nevada, where they were married in a Presbyterian parsonage. The minister's wife, daughter, and grandson were their witnesses. They only had a one-night honeymoon in Reno before returning to their respective homes, where they kept their marriage a secret.

Hawaiian brides wear seven strands of pikaki flowers, because it's a symbol of good luck.

When their parents found out about the wedding a month later, they "weren't all that happy," but finally, three months after the wedding, Erma's family had a shower for them where they passed out wedding announcements to the guests in attendance.

Throughout their 50 years of married life they struggled along, raising eight children. Times were very difficult at first as they lived with rationed tires, gasoline, sugar, meat, and shoes, something many of you reading this chapter know all about. Loren held many positions through the years: school bus driver, carpenter, contractor and, most recently, as owner of the Capital Door

Sales Company. Erma worked for the National Can Company, as well as the Census Bureau. She also helped in the family business as a secretary and bookkeeper.

They lost one of their children, their dear daughter, Nancy Lea, when she died in a single automobile accident in 1984, but their remaining seven children, plus their 21 grandchildren, seven great-grandchildren, and other family members and friends, honored them with a lovely 50th wedding anniversary celebration on December 30, 1995. There were 200 guests present to witness the reaffirmation of their vows. Five of their daughters and one granddaughter served as bridesmaids. Two sons and two grandsons served as groomsmen, and the rest of their grandchildren, great-grandchildren, and other family members all helped out. Loren and Erma have graciously allowed me to share the vow segment of their reaffirmation service with you.

Norma and Larry (Erma's sister and brother-in-law) delivered this reading that preceded their vows:

"The home is to provide the sweetest, most precious, and most endearing relationship on earth. The value can best be described by the words, 'sweeter as the years go by.' Marriage is a lifelong contract. It is not entered into thoughtlessly or lightly. Loren and Erma have realized that mind, heart, and soul have become one and they wish to renew their wedding vows to bind them the rest of their days. God has blessed this union as His word has been reverenced, loved, and relied on. Obedience to Him is the prime of their responsibilities. Consequently, they wish to create a bond of lasting love and devotion to each other for the rest of their days."

Minister: *"Please join hands and repeat after me:"*

Loren (repeating after the minister): *"I, Loren, promise to continue to love and cherish and protect Erma, whose hand I now hold, and provide for her in health and sickness, and be true to her, and cleave to her until death do us part. I renew my vow to take her for my lawful wedded wife."*

Erma (repeating after the minister): *"I, Erma, promise to continue to love and honor this man, Loren, whose hand I now hold, and be true and faithful to him and cleave to him until death do us part. I renew my vow to take him for my lawful wedded husband."*

Minister: *"I do by the virtue of authority vested in me as a minister of the gospel and the authority of the Father, sanction your desire to reaffirm your wedding vows."*

I wish I could include a photograph of Loren and Erma! If you could only see them, you would agree with me that they absolutely radiate with joy. Oh, that we could all look that good and be that happy after 50 years of married life!

❖ ❖ ❖

", I'm glad I had the good sense to marry you 50 years ago. They've been good years as we survived everything the world had to throw at us: those Depression years, when we made our own soap and ate by candlelight every night because we couldn't afford electricity; juggling two jobs at once when the children were growing up; those painful times of separation when I served in the Navy during the war; and the day we lost our stock in the range fire, We've been through a lot together, but our love has survived it all and we deserve to celebrate. I love you, my darling husband/wife , as much today as the I married you, and I'm happy to commit myself to you as your loving husband/wife for at least 50 more years!"

"*When we were married* _____ *years ago today, I thought I knew what love was. I was in love with you, that I knew for sure; but, as I look back on all our years together, I realize now that our love at its beginning, although it was real and sure, was only a shallow imitation of the love I feel for you today. Every year, in your precious way, you have made me love you more and more. And why? Because the more I know you, the more I love you. You are worthy of a deep, holy love, and that is what I feel for you today as I gladly recommit my heart and life to you.*"

"*On this day* _____ *years ago, I promised to love you and cherish you all the days of my life. I hereby reaffirm that promise, in the presence of God and our family.* _____, *you have been my friend and companion and the revered mother/father of our children, but, most of all, you have been my beautiful, loving wife/handsome, loving husband for all these years, and I renew my pledge to you today of my eternal devotion.*"

> *Marriage by capture was still legal in England until the middle of the 13th century.*

Reaffirmation vows with the wine ceremony

A wine ceremony can be a lovely way to add a special touch to your reaffirmation vows. The couple sips from the same glass or silver cup and then recites their vows. Some couples choose to use the same glasses they used during their wedding reception, but others arrange for special commemorative glasses.

"As we drink together from this cup of wine, so may we continue in a perfect union of love and devotion to each other as we continue to draw contentment, comfort, and felicity from the cup of life, and thereby find life's joys doubly gladdening and its bitterness sweetened by our true companionship and love."

When a Korean bride and groom marry, ducks are often used as symbols of a long and happy marriage, because ducks mate for life.

$\mathcal{C}$HAPTER SIX
VOWS FOR OLDER COUPLES

Personalized wedding vows carry special significance when a man or woman finds "the one" much later in life. Sometimes this happens after many years of searching, but other times it happens when a man or woman loses a longtime mate to death or divorce, and then finds another and marries again. Either way, a wedding for older couples should be just as special as those for the young. Here are several vow phrasings that were graciously contributed by older brides and grooms.

> It is a Belgian tradition for a bride to carry a handkerchief embroidered with her name when she gets married. It is framed and displayed in the couple's home, until the next family bride adds her name to the handkerchief and carries it down the aisle.

"_____, we have suffered much in this life, each in our own way, and what a miracle it is to find each other now, just when we need each other the most. I want to take care of you now, to be your shelter and your light, putting the past behind us as we face a joyous new life together for our remaining years. How I thank God for sending you to me, to stand beside me, to hold me and to share your life with me. I need you and I love you more than simple words can say. I pledge to you today, before our family and friends, with this holy vow of matrimony, to be your loving, true, and faithful partner, from this day forward."

"We have experienced the joys and sorrows of life through our many years on this earth. We have loved and married before and raised our families in the fear of the Lord. And then, in our twilight years, when we least expected it, God, in His divine providence, has brought us together with a love and a joy as fresh as our youth. How I thank God for bringing you to me, my friend, my companion, my precious jewel. I hereby pledge myself to be your faithful husband/wife with a love that will endure for all the rest of our days."

"_____, I vow to you this day to be your true and faithful husband/wife, and to erase your tears of sorrow, replacing them with the hope and promise of my love for you. I pledge to lift you up, set you on the highest mountain, and bring only goodness and joy to you all the days of your life."

An English bride and her wedding party traditionally walk together to the church, the procession led by a small girl who scatters blossoms along the path.

"_____, until you came into my life, my heart was hollow. But your love has filled my heart and made me whole. We have both shed tears of loneliness after the loss of our mates, but our love has chased those shadows away and brought gladness and rejoicing to our frightened souls. I pledge to you now my love for all time as I ask you to become my husband/wife. From this day forward I promise to love you with all my heart, withholding nothing."

"In the presence of the Lord God, our children, and our grand-children, I take you, _____, to be my wedded husband/wife. I promise to love you, honor you, and cherish you, in sickness and in health, in good times and in bad, so long as we both shall live. May the Lord bless us with many happy years together and may the peace of Christ live always in our hearts and in our home as we become one."

"Because of you, I'm no longer lonely. Because of you, my life is brand new. Because of you, my heart is singing. Because of you, there are no more sorrows, no more tears. Because of you, my days are filled with hope and excitement. I am young again, dear _____, all because of you. I need you now and always, every waking moment, and I freely and wholly give myself to you this day, to be your loving and faithful husband/wife, and to be true to you always, as long as the Lord gives us together in this life."

"_____, we are *God's children, not young in years, but infinitely young at heart, as we join together, in the presence of our family and friends, as man and wife. We both have assurance that it was God's will that we met and fell in love, and so it is with a grateful heart, that I, _____, take you, _____, this day as my husband/wife, that we may live together as partners for eternity. May we always seek God first in our marriage and thank Him daily for giving us the gift of each other.*"

"_____, *you have brought light into the darkness of my life, music to my quiet days, and laughter to my solemn nights. You have revived me and given wings to my heart. Just as the hawk flies high overhead on the wings of the wind, so I will soar on the promise of your love. I give you, from this day forward, the gift of myself, my love, and all that I am. I will fill up the wounds in your heart, just as you will fill mine. In good times or in bad, I will stand by your side, and I will die with my love for you still untarnished in my heart.*"

"*I choose you to be my wife/husband. You are the one I adore; you are the one I cherish; you are the one I honor. At this late time of my life, you have startled me out of a deep sleep with your unexpectedly beautiful love. I receive you into the very breath of my soul, to be the light of my life, to fill my glad heart with a joy beyond all imaginings. I will hold your heart tenderly in the palms of my hands, cherishing it, thanking God for it. I give myself to you this day and I promise to be faithful to you for as long as we both shall live.*"

"I take you this day as my wife/husband because you are my beloved, the one I have chosen to journey with me through my remaining days. You are my princess/prince, my companion, my lover, and my friend, and I promise that wherever our journey leads and whatever its outcome, I will love you, cherish you, and be faithful to you."

Russian couples are given two blessed loaves of bread on their wedding day. One is to be eaten, and the other is to be kept, ensuring a happy and prosperous marriage.

"You have brought me back from the dead, my sweet one. Just when everything seemed dark and hopeless, God sent you to me, my bright ray of life. Your beauty surrounds you, and the world is a better place because of your loving heart. It is beyond comprehension that I should be so blessed to be loved by you. You have made life worth living again and I thank God we will spend it together, sharing our constant love and devotion, soul mates, together at last. I hereby vow, humbly before God, in the presence of our friends and family, to be your faithful husband/wife in whatever circumstances life may bring us through all the years He allows us to live."

"My precious love, you have brought summer to the winter of my life. You are the sunshine after the storm, my glorious hope of a new day. What have I done to deserve such good fortune, such a prize as you? I haven't the words to express the joy you have brought into my life, and I wholly and unreservedly take you as my wife/husband on this, our wedding day. I promise to love you, honor you, cherish you, and respect you always, until death do us part."

"_____, I take you as my life's partner in marriage for all the days God shall yet give us to live on this earth. I promise to love you, honor you, praise you, care for you, serve you, listen to you, encourage you, and stand by you always, even in times of illness and crisis. I promise to laugh with you when you laugh, cry with you with you cry, and hold you fast beside me until the gates of death finally open and separate us."

> In the Phillippines, the wedding guests throw money at the feet of the bridal couple as they perform the traditional wedding dance, called the "ado."

Up close and personal

I would like to tell you about a couple who were married three years ago. They were ages 76 and 73 at the time. Horace and Emma were married to their first loves for more than 50 years, and both of them were caregivers to their mates until they both passed away.

Throughout their years of married life, the two couples were quite close, traveling together, square dancing together, and truly loving each other as dear friends.

When Horace and Emma each lost their mate, it seemed only natural for them to spend time together, consoling each other and trying to bear up under the weight of such a devastating loss.

Well, one thing led to another, and within six months or so, people noticed Horace and Emma holding hands and snuggling in public, so it wasn't surprising when they decided to get married. I was lucky enough to attend their wedding, and these were their eloquently written vows:

Horace: *"Emma, we have lived long, full lives and experienced many joys and sorrows. We have each raised our families in the fear and admonition of the Lord, releasing them finally to their own joys and sorrows to be found in this world. Then, when we lost our loving mates and our hearts were full of pain, God brought us to each other so that we may find joy again. And what a joy you are to me, my precious Emma, my dear one, God's gift to me. I'm so thankful for you, and I give myself to you this day, freely and without reservation, as I vow to be your loving, faithful husband for all the days we have left together on this earth."*

Emma: *"We have lived long lives, and we wouldn't trade our lives for any prize the world could offer, but, because of you, life is more precious to me today than it has ever been before. You have brought me a joy and fresh anticipation of a happy new life yet to come as I take you as my husband. As we stand here before our friends and family, our children and grandchildren, I publicly declare my love for you. I want them to know how proud I am of you and how special our love is. I give myself to you, Horace, on this our wedding day, and I promise to be your faithful wife for all the years that God may give us together on this earth."*

Soon after the wedding Horace and Emma moved to Missouri to be closer to their children, but they were recently back in California to attend the funeral of one of their close friends, and I overheard Horace (now 79 years old, mind you) as he confided to one of his old buddies at the reception that followed: "I'm telling you, Harry, she's an awful lot of fun when the sun goes down, if you know what I mean."

I glanced at Emma to see if she may have overheard his remark. She had, and was blushing like a new bride.

In Mexico, the bride and groom kneel before the altar as they each hold a lighted candle and the priest wraps a single silver cord around them, uniting them in marriage.

CHAPTER SEVEN
VOWS WITH RELIGIOUS VARIATIONS

Many couples want their vows to have deep spiritual meaning, reflecting their personal faith in God, as well as their religious heritage. This chapter includes many of these vows, with several different phrasings from which to choose. Most vows are based on scripture, prayer, or the religious commitment of the bride and groom.

"I take you, _____, as my lawfully wedded husband/wife according to God's holy ordinance. I feel blessed beyond words and favored beyond measure that God brought you into my life. I promise to be faithful to you, giving you honor, respect, and understanding as we strive to live in harmony and humility, in times of great or plenty, sickness or health, knowing that our marriage has been sanctioned by God and that our lives are fully entrusted to Him."

> When the Orthodox Jewish groom crushes a glass under his foot during the marriage ceremony, he metaphorically enacts his union with his bride. At the same time, he recalls the destruction of the Jewish Temple in Jerusalem.

105

❖❖❖

"_____, you are my beloved bride/groom, whom I choose to marry this day. I know that marriage is a holy union, instituted by God in the Garden of Eden when He saw that it was not good for man to live alone. Marriage was also given a crown of glory by the Apostle Paul, who likened it to that Holy union which exists between Christ and His church. I come into this holy relationship this day to be joined with you, _____, as your lawfully wedded husband/wife. I pray that our hearts will be joined together by the holy seal of God's approval as we become one."

❖❖❖

"_____, I promise to be your faithful husband/wife, loving you and serving you with all my heart, just as my heart also longs to love and serve God. I enter into this holy estate of matrimony with great reverence, soberly and discreetly, in the fear of God, realizing that marriage is instituted by Him, signifying the mystical union that is between Christ and His church. And just as Christ gave Himself for His church, so I give myself unreservedly to you on this, our wedding day."

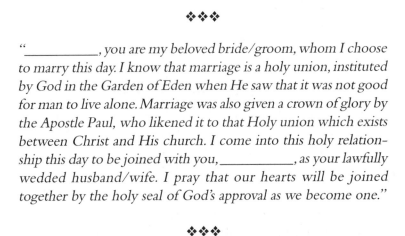

The Japanese bride and groom take sips of saké, a Japanese wine, in the "san-san-kudi" (three and three, nine times) ceremony, becoming husband and wife after the first sip.

"_____, I commit my love to you this day for as long as we both shall live. This love is the very flame of God, and may no man dare to quench it. I promise to be faithful to you, to nurture you, to cherish you, and encourage you, with the same care and concern that I give myself. I promise to help you become all the man/woman our Lord has intended you to be. Throughout our lifetime together, you will always be my beloved husband/wife and my best friend."

"It is the deepest desire of my heart and the holy will of God Almighty that I give myself to you as your husband/wife, to walk with you in riches or poverty, in sickness or in health, in good times or bad. I will always stand by your side, praying for you, supporting you, and encouraging you, and I will always seek to communicate with you, never holding anything back, so that we may be one unified spirit, until death do us part."

"_____, I come to you this day in holy reverence as I take you as my husband/wife. I thank God that He, in His holy providence, has given us to each other. My prayer is that our hearts will be melded together this day with God's seal of approval and that I will be a good and faithful husband/wife, always providing you with emotional and spiritual nourishment, supporting you in every way. May we live together in such a way that it will be evident to all that we have a deep, abiding love for each other, and for our God and Heavenly Father. May God bless our marriage for all our days."

Groom (to his bride): "_____, God, our Father, is the one who established marriage. It was His plan, and therefore it is only with His help and blessing that we dare take this great step in our lives. My prayer is that I will be a husband worthy of your praise, your faithful provider and protector, and your haven from harm. I promise to be tender, understanding, and true to you always, for all the days God may give us on this earth."

Bride (to her groom): "_____, I have an abiding faith in God, and I, too, take this great step of marriage with reverence. I promise to hold fast to my faith in Him and in you, as my dear husband. I realize that marriage is not merely the act of living together and pleasing each other, but of living for God and pleasing Him, and I pray that He will give us a great spiritual purpose in our life together."

❖❖❖

"_____, it is with unspeakable joy that I take you to be my wedded wife/husband, and that together we may become one. As Christ loves His Body, the Church, so I promise to love you with an unselfish devotion. I will care for you with all my tenderness and I will always seek to strengthen you, comfort you, encourage you, and hold you up daily in prayer before our Heavenly Father. I pledge you my faithfulness and eternal love from this day forward."

❖❖❖

Bride: "I, _____, take you, _____, as my husband."

Groom: "I, _____, take you, _____, as my wife."

Bride: "I promise to be a faithful wife."

Groom: "I promise to be a faithful husband."

Bride: *"May our life together be a sign of Christ's love to a broken world."*

Groom: *"May our deep, abiding love for each other be a sign of our everlasting bond."*

Bride: *"May we each be strength to the other."*

Groom: *"And may we seek to comfort in sorrow and be companions in joy."*

Bride: *"May we accept our faults."*

Groom: *"And seek each other's forgiveness."*

Bride: *"May God bless our marriage covenant."*

Korean couples make their marriage vows silently as they bow to one another, in a sign of deep respect and reverence.

Groom: *"And may our lives be lived in the fullness of His love, for now, and forever."*

Bride: *"May our lives be lived in the fullness of His love, for now, and forever."*

Up close and personal

When Warren and Verna told me how they met and fell in love, I decided their story was as poignant as any romantic movie script ever written. Verna was a 33-year-old schoolteacher who owned her own home and 19 acres of productive grapevines. Her life was full and satisfying, except for one thing: She was still looking for "Mr. Right."

Along came Warren, a man in his mid-30s, the "new guy in town" who planned to enroll at the local university in the fall. Warren met Verna one Sunday at church, and it soon became known that he, being the typically destitute American college student, needed a job if he was to survive the summer and have enough money to enroll for the fall semester.

The summer work season was just beginning at Verna's vineyard and, of course, it was perfectly understandable that she needed help with the annual weeding, so Warren offered to help her pull the weeds, if she would promise to cook him one home-cooked meal per day. As Warren labored shoulder to shoulder with Verna under the hot California sun, it was only natural that he worked up a thirst. So, of course, it was only logical for Verna to join him for a cold lemonade. And, of course, a man can't work straight through the day without a little rest in the shade. And, of course, it was only logical for Verna to join him occasionally. After all, it isn't polite to leave a guy sitting all alone.

Well, after a few dozen jugs of lemonade, many hours visiting under the shade of the big oak tree, and plate after plate of good home cooking, they realized that they had fallen in love. By that September they were engaged to be married. They knew in their hearts that God had brought them together that summer, and their personalized wedding vows reflected this assurance.

Minister: *"Will you, Warren, have Verna to be your lawfully wedded wife, and do you solemnly promise that you will loyally fulfill your obligations as her husband, to protect her, to honor her, and to cherish her in adversity as well as in prosperity, and to keep yourself unto her alone so long as you both shall live?"*

Warren: *"I will."*

Minister: *"Will you, Verna, have Warren to be your lawfully wedded husband, and do you solemnly promise that you will be unto him a tender, loving and true wife, in sunshine and shadow alike, and to be faithful to him so long as you both shall live?"*

Verna: *"I will."*

Warren/Verna: *"_____, I acknowledge God's presence in our lives and I believe that He has led us together to share our lives with each other, so I pledge to you my undying love, my respect, my devotion, and my life, without reservation, from this moment on. I promise that, with God's help, I will be a faithful, loving husband/wife, and that whether times are easy or hard, I will always remember that each of us is meant for the other, with Christ at the head of our home."*

By the way, Verna still teaches school and they live in her home on the 19 acres where Warren is now a full-time dairy farmer. She's still feeding him pretty well, and if you should happen to drive out their country road some warm summer afternoon, you'll probably find them sharing a lemonade under the shade of that same old oak tree.

❖ ❖ ❖

"_____, this is our happy day, the day we have been looking forward to for so long, the day we become husband and wife, united through Christ, in holy matrimony. I know that our deep and abiding love for each other comes from God above, for God is love, and I know that this love is to be nurtured, cherished, and developed every day as we draw

The godparents of a Mexican bride and groom offer a prayer book, rosary, and kneeling pillow for the marriage ceremony.

closer to each other. This is a sacred moment in our lives, because marriage is holy, and I enter the estate of marriage with great reverence. I promise to be your pillar of strength and your haven from harm, your protector and your greatest supporter, and I will be your true and faithful husband/wife for all the days of our lives."

"I promise to be a faithful husband/wife, to care for you in loving devotion, to be your strength when you are in need, to be your counselor in your perplexity, to be your comfort in sorrow, to be your companion in joy. I promise to pray for you, uphold you, defend you, and to seek your forgiveness if I should ever hurt you in any way. I make this vow before our family, our friends, and before God."

"_____, you are God's perfect gift to me, an unspeakable blessing to my life. In my wildest dreams I could have never imagined someone as dear and precious as you, someone I could love so deeply and with such total devotion. Just as God gave Eve to Adam as his helpmate, so that he would be complete, so God has given you to me. I vow to try, with God's help, to be everything He wants me to be for you. I want to be your comforter, your helper, your encourager, your provider, and your servant. As we begin our life together today as husband and wife, I gladly lay down all my rights, so that I can be to you everything you need. May God bless our marriage and make us pleasing to Him."

112

"_____, I take you as my lawfully wedded husband/wife, and I hereby pledge myself to be faithful, an example of Christ's love in our home. May our lives together as a married couple be a sign of His love and concern for the world. I give myself wholly to you this hour, and I promise to guard, cherish, and protect you all the days of my life. May our home be blessed by our love for one another, and br Christ's love for us."

"I, _____, take you, _____, as my cherished husband. It is the greatest desire of my heart to be faithful to you and to love you always, seeking to meet your every need, desiring to help you in every way, listening to you, encouraging you, comforting you, and standing by your side in whatever circumstances may face us in the years ahead. I will respect you, honor you, and strive for harmony in our marriage with a quiet and gentle spirit. As God created Eve for Adam, so I shall be a helper to you always, from this day forth, and for as long as we both shall live."

"_____, because of our faith in God and our assurance that He has brought us together, I come to this ceremony in reverence and awe. I vow to be a faithful husband/wife to you. I promise to put God first in our marriage, depending on him for guidance and wisdom, as we seek His will in our married life. I realize that marriage, like our creation as man and woman, owes its very existence to God, and so I take this commitment seriously. I come into this holy union without reservation and I give myself to you for companionship, help, and comfort, in prosperity or in adversity, for all the days of our lives."

"_____, as marriage has been established by God, I willingly bind myself to you this day in love, even as Christ is one with the Church. Just as nothing can separate us from the love of God in Christ, nothing can separate us as husband and wife, as I pledge the same steadfast love to you. I promise, with God's help, to be your faithful husband/wife, to love and serve you as Christ commands, as long as we both shall live."

"_____, because God has given you to me as my own, I also give myself to you this day. I promise to be a patient and tolerant husband/wife, to forgive freely, as our Lord has forgiven us, and, above everything else, to be truly loving, faithful, and thankful. My love for you will outlast everything. It will stand when all else has fallen. I promise this as a solemn vow before God and these witnesses."

"_____, you are God's priceless gift to me. You are my beloved, my friend, my dove, my perfect one. Your voice is sweet. Put me like a seal over your heart. I take you as my wife/husband from this day forward, to join with you and share our lives together, and be true to you with my whole being. My commitment is made in love, to be kept in faith, lived in hope and eternally made new."

"We are here today because of a miracle, the miracle of our love. I come to you with a pure heart as I commit myself to you as your husband/wife. I promise to walk with you from this day forward as your life partner, always searching for God's will in our lives, and trusting Him for His blessings. He may bless our union with children, and if we are so blessed, we will praise Him for yet another miracle of love in our lives."

❖❖❖

"_____, I believe that marriage is ordained by God, and so today I marry you in the spirit of Christian joy to become united with you as one. Our lives have been touched by His love, a love as soft as the dawn, as radiant as the sun, as bright as the moon, and as beautiful as the rainbow that enfolds us after a storm. I give you my heart this day. Open your heart and lock mine inside. I give you my life. Open yours and let me become one with you. Just as the flower opens to the warmth of the sun, so shall our marriage blossom as it basks in the warmth of our love. May this love be always bright, always beautiful, and always new. This is the first day of our life together."

❖❖❖

Minister: "Do you, _____, promise your Heavenly Father to take _____, to be your wife/husband, to love and care for him/her, in the good that may light your way, and in the misfortunes that may darken your day, and to be true to him/her in all circumstances until death alone shall part you?"

Bride/Groom: "I do."

❖❖❖

Bride: "The ever-blessed God Almighty has brought us together by His providence."

Groom: "He has enriched us with His grace and sanctified us by His Spirit."

Bride: *"Today is the day our lives will be changed forever."*

Groom: *"From this day forward, we will cherish each other as husband and wife."*

Bride: *"We will hold each other with mutual esteem and love."*

Groom: *"We will always bear with each other's infirmities and weaknesses."*

Bride: *"We will always comfort each other in sickness, trouble, and sorrow."*

Groom: *"We will pray for each other and encourage each other."*

Bride: *"We will surprise each other with the joy, wonder, and miracle of marriage."*

Groom: *"We will be always warm to each other with affection and laughter."*

Bride: *"Our love will bear all things and believe all things."*

Groom: *"Our love will hope all things and endure all things."*

Bride: *"Our love will outlast everything."*

Groom: *"We will love each other forever, just as we love each other this day."*

Bride: *"Just as we do today, our wedding day."*

"Before God brought you into my life, I walked alone. Now I have you at my side and we walk together. You are my strength and my priceless treasure. I cherish you, adore you, and thank

God for you. Just as the Bible says that God dwells in us and his love is perfected in us, so God knew us both and chose us from the beginning of time, to share as one and to be one. I welcome you, _____, as my husband/wife, and I promise with God's help to be your faithful husband/wife, to love and serve you as Christ commands, as long as we both shall live."

> In rural China, the groom's family brings gifts to the bride's family in large wedding baskets filled with oranges, chickens, cakes, and roasted pig.

❖❖❖

"_____, I give myself to you as your husband/wife, to join with you and be true to you with my whole being. My heart is open and my soul rejoices to God as we become one. I promise to love you for all the days of my life, in my waking and in my sleeping, in joy or sadness, so help me God."

❖❖❖

"I love you, _____, and before our God, our family, and our friends, I lovingly take you to be my husband/wife and I give myself to you. I give you all that I am, all that I have, and all that I will ever be. Just as Jesus Christ has loved me with an unconditional love, so shall I love you. I will always seek to communicate with you in honesty and with total respect for your opinions, seeking your happiness and best interests in life. And just as God forgives me, so shall I forgive you and love you as I love myself. I promise to keep our love fresh, never allowing it to stagnate, seeking to express my love for you in some way every day. I hereby give myself, totally, unreservedly, and eternally, for as long as we shall live together on this earth."

Bride: *"We are soul mates. I'm so blessed to have found you at last, after searching for so long."*

Groom: *"Yes, we are soul mates, and my life is now complete because of you."*

Bride: *"Because of you, there is melody in my life."*

Groom: *"Because of you, my life is filled with song."*

Bride: *"I thank God for you, and I give myself freely to you as your wife."*

Groom: *"I praise God for you, and I give myself freely to you as your husband."*

Bride: *"I have no doubts, no reservations."*

Groom: *"And I have none. In fact, I give my heart to you today with pure abandonment."*

Bride: *"My commitment to you is eternal."*

Groom: *"As is mine to you, from this day forth, so help me God."*

"I come to you today, before this company of witnesses, to join with you in holy matrimony, as your faithful husband/wife. I promise to be true to you always, forsaking all others, as I give you all that I am and all that I will ever be. May our marriage be always protected by God's love and may no one ever disturb our union. May God bless our marriage."

Bride: *"God blessed me the day I found you."*

Groom: *"And you are God's indescribable gift to me."*

Bride: *"You give purpose to my life."*

Groom: *"And you make each day a special day for me."*

Bride: *"Thank for for being the love of my life."*

Groom: *"Thank you for being my sweetheart, my darling."*

Bride: *"There is nothing more important in my life than your happiness. This is proof of my true love for you."*

Groom: *"And my true love for you is demonstrated by my promise to care for you always, putting you first in my life."*

Bride: *"I want to share my life with you. I want you there at my side to face all the joys and despairs of the future."*

Groom: *"I promise to be there for you always, to help you, comfort you, encourage you, and lift you up, no matter what the circumstances."*

Bride: *"I give myself to you with joy, to be your faithful wife and the mother of your children. Please accept my love."*

Groom: *"I give myself to you with joy, to be your faithful husband and the father of our children. Please accept my love."*

Up close and personal

On July 29, 1995, my husband and I had the privilege of attending the wedding of Colleen and Joel. What made this wedding extra-special was not only that they wrote their own poignant wedding vows, but that they had waited seven long years, determined to graduate from college before getting married. They were high school sweethearts, of course, and graduated together from university.

Colleen: *"Joel, I stand before you today, honored and excited as I am about to become your wife. I thank the Lord for the enduring and patient love He has given us these past seven years. You are a loving, gentle, and kind man. You're devoted and committed to serving others and the Lord. You are the love of my life, and I am so blessed with the gift of spending the rest of my life with you. As we become husband and wife today, I promise to love you with an unending and unconditional love. I will honor and respect you; comfort and cherish you. May I bring you good, not harm, all the days of my life. I will stand by*

> In Switzerland, the youngest bridesmaid leads the procession to the reception with a basket full of colored handkerchiefs for the wedding guests.

you and submit to you as God guides us to do His will. I will be with you in sickness and in health, whether we are rich or poor, and during the times when we are filled with joy or when we are filled with sorrow. I will not leave you. Joel, I will be yours alone as long as God allows us to live."

Joel: "Today, I have come to commit my love to you. Although I come with a fallible love, I promise to strive to love you as Christ has loved the church. I promise to cherish you in times of joy and despair, to care for you when you are sick and in health, to hope with you now and forever, to protect you and not to harm you, to love you and to forsake all others. I promise to love you as scripture commands me to, 'for love is patient, love is kind. It does not envy, it does not boast, it is not proud. Love does not delight in evil, but rejoices with the truth. It always protects, always hopes, always perseveres. Where there are prophecies, they will cease; where there are tongues, they will be stilled; where there is knowledge, it will pass away, but love...love never fails. And now these three remain: Faith, Hope, and Love, but the greatest of these is Love.' Although calamity and darkness may surround us, I promise to be here when you need me. Although the world values 'being in love,' I promise to love you even if the feelings of love go away. Before our friends and family, before you, and before my Lord and Savior, I commit these promises to you."

Joel and Colleen are presently teaching in Southern California, and when I spoke to them recently on the telephone they sounded very happy.

Vows for the Christian ministry

"_____, as we go forward from this, our wedding day, into God's service, I give you the love of my heart, and I promise to be a loving and faithful husband/wife, with thanks to God whose gift of love has brought us together and lifted us up to serve Him together in joy and gladness. Our union is a holy union as we become one, husband and wife, joined together by God's ordinance of holy matrimony. How blessed we are to have found each other and God's holy will for our lives. I promise to love you, _____, to honor and cherish you, from this day forward. Our service may bring many hardships and disappointments, but together we will be strong in the Lord and faithful to each other, upholding each other in prayer, always ready to comfort and encourage. Our service will bring many joys, as well, and this too, we will share in common praise and thanksgiving to our Lord who has us always in the palm of His hand."

"_____, God has called us to serve Him together and as I take you today as my husband/wife, my first priority is my own relationship with God, to be right with Him and to have the assurance of being in His will. I know this is the first priority in your life, as well. But after my commitment to God comes my total devotion to you as I become your husband/wife. You have been blessed with many abilities and gifts, and I promise to encourage you as you develop these God-given talents. I promise to support you in your ministry as you seek to serve Him. I will pray for you and encourage you in your Christian walk so that you will be free to be all He wants you to be. I will love you, care for you, sacrifice for you, and be faithful to you from this day forward and for all the years to come. May God bless our marriage and our ministry together."

"_____, I promise to be your faithful husband/wife, loving you and serving you with all my heart, just as my heart also longs to love and serve God. I enter into this holy estate of matrimony with great reverence, soberly and discreetly, in the fear of God, realizing that marriage is instituted by Him, signifying the mystical union that is between Christ and His church. And just as Christ gave Himself for His church, so I give myself unreservedly to you on this, our wedding day."

Vows based on a traditional Protestant prayer

"I thank the Almighty God, our heavenly Father, the fountain of all our joy, for giving you to me. I pledge my sacred vow to walk with you in love, to rejoice in the bond of marriage, to carry the inspiration of this hour with me the rest of my life, whether there is joy or sorrow, whether there are pleasant days or trials. I will be a comfort and a joy to you always; I will be your counsel and strength as we walk together along the pathway of life in faith, hope, and love."

Vows based on the Episcopalian declaration of intent

"I vow to be your faithful husband/wife, understanding that marriage is a lifelong union, and not to be entered into lightly, for the purpose of mutual fellowship, encouragement, and understanding, and for the procreation of children and their physical and spiritual nurture. I hereby give myself to you in this cause with my sacred vow before God."

Interfaith weddings

Interfaith weddings have become commonplace in our country, naturally resulting in many variations of the traditional religious wedding vows. An interfaith service may be conducted by a clergyperson sympathetic to the individual faiths of the bride and groom, or the service may be purely ecumenical with two officiants, one representing the bride and one the groom. In some cases it isn't possible for an interfaith marriage to be officially sanctioned at all. Orthodox and Conservative Jewish rabbis, for example, usually refuse to officiate at a mixed marriage.

The Roman Catholic attitude is usually that, on a case-by-case basis, it is possible for a Catholic to marry a non-Catholic, but only under certain conditions. For example, in such a marriage the Catholic groom may be required to promise, either in writing or orally, that he will do all in his power to share the Catholic faith with any children that may result from the union. He must also promise that the children will be baptized and reared as Roman Catholics.

There are multitudes of rules and restrictions within Protestant denominations as well. These rules not only vary from one denomination to the other, but from one congregation to another. For example, a divorced person usually may not be married within the Episcopal faith, except by special permission.

In order for a couple to be married in a Quaker wedding service, at least one of the couple must be a member of the Religious Society of Friends. The restrictions are so varied that it is wise to set an appointment with the clergyperson of the particular church you have chosen before making further plans.

Jewish/Christian interfaith

A typical Jewish-Christian wedding ceremony is conducted by co-officiants. Here are the wedding vows used recently in one of these services:

"I, _____, take you, _____, to be my wedded wife/ husband. I promise and covenant, before God and all these witnesses, to be your loving and faithful husband/wife, in plenty and in want, in joy and in sorrow, in sickness and in health, as long as we both shall live."

❖❖❖

Or this simpler version may also be used:

"Do you, _____, take _____ to be your lawfully wedded wife/husband, and do you promise to love, honor, and cherish him/her as long as you shall live/love?"

Catholic/Non-Catholic interfaith

The wedding of a Catholic and a non-Catholic usually includes this vow:

"I, _____, take you, _____, to be my wife/husband. I promise to be true to you in good times and in bad, in sickness and in health. I will love you and honor you all the days of my life."

Catholic/Jewish interfaith

This type of wedding service is usually co-officiated by a priest and a rabbi. The wedding vows can vary, but usually include an

Introduction (by the priest or rabbi). Often the bride and groom compose their own vows or incorporate phrasings from the traditional Catholic and Jewish services. A common alternative is as follows:

"_____, I accept you as my wife/husband and call upon the Jewish and Christian communities to witness our union."

Messianic Jew/Christian interfaith

This is the marriage of a Jew who believes in Yeshua (Jesus) and a gentile Christian. These ceremonies usually incorporate all the traditional Jewish marriage rituals and are conducted by a rabbi. This type of service differs from the Orthodox, Conservative, or Reformed Jewish marriage ceremonies, however, because of the couple's belief that Yeshua, Jesus of Nazareth, is the Messiah and the King of the Jews.

Up close and personal

I am acquainted with a Messianic Jew/Christian couple, Andrew and Karen, members of the Ahavat Zion Messianic Synagogue in Beverly Hills, who were married at the Chateau Bradbury in California by their rabbi. Many Messianic Jewish synagogues throughout the United States conduct their services on the Sabbath, according to Jewish tradition.

Andrew and Karen have a fascinating love story. They first met over the computer bulletin board when they both attended the University of Southern California. They communicated via their computers for two years before finally meeting in person. Karen is now an instructional designer, and Andrew plans to teach.

They have kindly provided me with a copy of their rabbi's notes for the wedding sermon, as well as the details of their service, including the wording for the exchange of their rings and vows and the Seven Blessings that were read in both Hebrew and English.

Rabbi (to Andrew): *"Andrew, son of Karl and Patricia, may your house and the household of G-d increase. Do you attest, that after prayer and due consideration to know the will of G-d for your life, that the G-d of Israel, Blessed be He, has moved you to take this woman at your side to be your bride?"*

Andrew: *"I do."*

Rabbi: *"Do you promise to uphold her, devoting yourself to her welfare and nurture, encouraging her in her walk with G-d, conscious that by her service to G-d, He would have her submit herself to you as her husband in love and faith?"*

Andrew: *"I do."*

Rabbi: *"What token do you offer as a sign or symbol of your love for her in the sight of G-d? Place the ring on her finger and repeat after me:*

Harei at mikudeshet li

B'taba'aat zu

k'da'at Elohei Yisrael."

(Translated as:

With this ring

You are consecrated to me

According to the ordinance of G-d of Israel.)

Rabbi (to Karen): *"Karen, daughter of Larry and Judy, may the L-rd make you like Sarah and Rebekkah, like Rachael and Leah. Do you attest that after prayer and consideration to know the will of G-d for your life, that the G-d of Israel, Blessed by He, has moved you join your life to that of this man, to be his bride?"*

Karen: *"I do."*

Rabbi: *"Do you promise to honor him as your husband, submitting to him, and helping him in every way to grow in submission to the will of G-d?"*

Karen: *"I do."*

Rabbi: *"What token do you offer as a sign or symbol of your love for him in the sight of G-d? Place the ring on his finger and repeat after me:*

Harei at mikudeshet li

B'taba'aat zu

k'da'at Elohei Yisrael.

(Translated as:

With this ring

You are consecrated to me

According to the ordinance of G-d of Israel.)

"The Seven Blessings:

"You Abound in Blessings, Adonai our G-d, who creates the fruit of the vine.

"You Abound in Blessings, Adonai our G-d. You created all things for Your glory.

"You Abound in Blessings, Adonai our G-d. You created humanity.

"You Abound in Blessings, Adonai our G-d. You made human-kind in Your image, after Your likeness, and You prepared from us a perpetual relationship. You Abound in Blessings, Adonai our G-d, You created humanity.

"May she who was barren rejoice when her children are united in her midst in joy. You Abound in Blessings, Adonai our G-d, who makes Zion rejoice with her children.

"You make these beloved companions greatly rejoice even as You rejoiced in Your creation in the Garden of Eden as of old. You Abound in Blessings, Adonai our G-d, who makes the bridegroom and bride to rejoice.

"You Abound in Blessings, Adonai our G-d, who created joy and gladness, bridegroom and bride, mirth and exultation, pleasure and delight, love, fellowship, peace and friendship. Soon may there be heard in the cities of Judah and in the streets of Jerusalem, the voice of joy and gladness, the voice of the bridegroom and the voice of the bride, the jubilant voice of the bridegrooms from their canopies and of youths from their feast of song as the Messiah who is the eternal bridegroom to all who trust Him returns to gather Jacob's children from every corner of the earth. You Abound in Blessings, Adonai our G-d, You make the bridegroom rejoice with the bride."

These Seven Blessings are almost identical to the traditional Seven Blessings already given in Chapter 1 in the section on Jewish ceremonies; the important difference is the mention of the Messiah in the seventh blessing where He is referred to as the "eternal bridegroom to all who trust Him."

> During a Jewish wedding, the ring is first placed on the right forefinger of the bride, which is known as the finger of intelligence, as it is used to point out the letters when reading the Torah.

CHAPTER EIGHT
RING VOWS

The wedding ring is seen as a seal upon the wedding vow, a symbol of the couple's lifetime commitment to one another. It is also seen by some to be a religious symbol of the holiness and sacredness of marriage. Whatever your beliefs, the giving and receiving of rings has been universally associated with marriage and weddings since Roman times.

This chapter contains a variety of ring vows, some traditional, and some non-traditional, since it has become popular for the bride and groom to write their own personalized ring vows, as well as the wedding vows themselves.

The Assyrians and Egyptians gave a sandal as a token of good faith when purchasing land. It eventually became a British custom for a father to give his son-in-law one of the bride's shoes, signifying the transfer of authority.

Jewish

Rabbi (addressing the bridegroom): *"Then, do you, _____, put this ring upon the finger of your bride and say to her: 'Be thou consecrated to me, as my wife, by this ring, according to the Law of Moses and of Israel.'"*

The Rabbi then asks the bride to repeat the following:

"May this ring I receive from thee be a token of my having become thy wife according to the Law of Moses and of Israel."

If two rings are used, the bride may say:

"This ring is a symbol that thou art my husband in accordance with the Law of Moses and Israel."

Catholic

The priest blesses the rings:

"Blessing of the Wedding Rings

Our help is in the name of the Lord,

Who made heaven and earth.

O Lord, hear my prayer.

And let my cry come unto Thee.

The Lord be with you.

And with your spirit."

Priest (to the couple): "Now that you have sealed a truly Christian marriage, give these wedding rings to each other, saying after me:"

Groom (addressing his bride): "In the name of the Father, and of the Son, and of the Holy Spirit. Take and wear this ring as a pledge of my fidelity."

Bride (addressing her bridegroom): *"In the name of the Father, and of the Son, and of the Holy Spirit. Take and wear this ring as a pledge of my fidelity."*

Evangelical Lutheran

"I give you this ring as a sign of my love and faithfulness."

Episcopalian

Groom/bride: *"_____, I give you this ring as a symbol of my vow, and with all that I am, and all that I have, I honor you, in the Name of the Father, and of the Son, and of the Holy Spirit (or 'in the Name of God')."*

Presbyterian

"This ring I give you, in token and pledge, of our constant faith, and abiding love."

"With this ring I thee wed, in the name of the Father, and of the Son, and of the Holy Spirit. Amen."

> *Islam, one of the world's leading religions, has no formal or traditional marriage ceremony.*

Methodist

"_____, I give you this ring as a sign of my vow, and with all that I am, and all that I have, I honor you."

> An English bride is considered lucky if she has been kissed by a chimney sweep.

United Church of Christ

"This ring I give you in token of my faithfulness and love, and as a pledge to honor you with my whole being and to share with you my worldly goods."

"I give you this ring in token of the covenant made today between us; in the name of the Father, and of the Son, and of the Holy Spirit."

"I give you this ring in token of the covenant made today. In the name of the Father, I will share with you my worldly goods."

United Church of Canada

"_____, I give you this ring that you may wear it as a symbol of our marriage."

Unitarian/Universalist

The minister repeats these words as the rings are exchanged between the bride and groom:

"As a token of mutual fidelity and affection the ring(s) are now given and received."

The bride and groom, if they wish, may repeat their own ring vows:

"With this ring, I wed you and pledge you my love now and forever."

"Be consecrated to me, with this ring, as my wife/husband in accordance with the faith of our loved ones."

Jewish/Christian

"Be thou consecrated unto me, as my love, with this ring, as my wife/husband, according to the faith of God and humanity."

Nondenominational

"I offer you this ring as a sign of my love and fidelity. It will always be a symbol of the vows which have made us husband and wife here this morning."

"I accept this ring as a symbol of our love and wear it proudly as your wife."

"Dear _____, with this ring I thee wed, and by it be thou consecrated unto me, as my lawfully wedded wife/husband according to the laws of God and of man."

"With this ring I wed you and pledge my faithful love. I take you as my husband/wife and pledge to share my life openly with you, to speak the truth to you in love. I promise to honor and tenderly care for you, to cherish and encourage your fulfillment as an individual through all the changes of our lives."

"Now, may I have a token of your sincerity that you will keep these vows? From the beginning of time, the ring has symbolized many kinds of human relationships. Kings wore them to express their imperial authority; friends exchanged them as expressions of their good will; graduates wore them as expressions of their school loyalties. This simple band of gold, however, has come to its highest significance as a symbol of a marriage relationship. Wearing it bears witness to your marital fidelity."

A Mien wedding is preceded by the slaughter of a pig, which is then eaten during the wedding feast, a ritual symbolizing the agreement reached between the two families.

Minister (to the groom): "Do you, _____, give this ring to _____ as a token of your love for her?"

Groom: *"I do."*

Minister (to the bride): *"Will you, _____, take this ring from _____ as a token of his love for you, and will you wear it as an expression of your love for him?"*

Bride: *"I will."*

Minister (to the bride): *"Do you, _____, give this ring to _____ as an expression of your love for him?"*

Bride: *"I do."*

Minister (to the groom): *"Will you, _____, take this ring from _____ as a token of her love for you, and will you wear it as an expression of your love for her?"*

Groom: *"I will."*

"I bring this ring as a symbol of my love and fidelity as your husband/wife, and as I slide it onto your finger, I commit my very heart and soul to you, my dear husband/wife, and I ask you to wear it as a reminder of the vows we have taken today."

"With this ring I thee wed, in the Name of God. Amen."

"With this ring I wed thee and I accept thee as my husband/wife; I take thee as my partner in life and I hereby endow thee with all my worldly goods."

"May this ring be a permanent reminder of our holy promises and steadfast love, through Jesus Christ our Lord. Amen."

"_____, this ring is the sign of my love and faithfulness, and I give it to you in the name of the Father, the Son, and the Holy Spirit. Amen."

"Thou art my true beloved and I give thee this ring as a visible reminder to you and all who see it that my love for you is constant and eternal."

"You are my life, my love, my best friend. With this ring I wed thee. May it be a reminder of my true love and the sacred commitment I have made here today."

"When we were in high school, I gave you my class ring and you wore it on a chain around your neck to show the world that we were going steady. But today I give you something much more precious: a wedding ring. May it be a sign to all who see it that we're going steady for the rest of our lives and that you belong to me alone."

"As this ring encircles your finger from this day forward, year in and year out, so will my love forever encircle you. Wear this ring as a symbol of this love."

"With this ring I seal the loving commitment I have made to
you today. May you wear it proudly as my loving wife/
husband."

> Tradition says that the bride should
> send each guest home with a touch of
> her good fortune. Hence, "favors" are
> given to modern wedding guests.

"_____, take this ring as a seal upon the marriage vows I
have spoken and, as you wear it, may it be a reminder of how
much I love you, not only on this precious day, but every single
day of your life."

"This ring is the visible evidence of our invisible love; it symbolizes the joining of our spirits in sacred holy matrimony."

"As I place this ring on your finger, its perfect symmetry is a symbol of our perfect love. It has no beginning and no ending, a
symbol of the eternal commitment we have made to each other
today."

"Our love is even more precious than this diamond (or whatever stone the bride wears in her engagement ring), and more enduring than this band of gold, but I place this band on your finger as a symbol of our love and the vows we have spoken here today."

"Just as this ring is made from precious metal, sturdy and strong, so will our marriage be: a precious commitment to each other that remains sturdy and strong until death do us part."

"This ring is enduring evidence of my enduring love, and its purity is a symbol of the sacredness of our vows."

"Today we are on a mountaintop. Everything is good and happy and right. But someday there will be valleys, and as we walk together, may this ring be a reminder of this mountaintop experience and the vows we have made this day."

The kiss became part of the wedding ceremony as far back as Roman times, when it signified a legal bond that sealed contracts.

"Just as our love is shining and pure, so is this golden wedding ring, an emblem of the lifelong commitment I have made to you this day."

"With this ring I wed you. Not only for today, our wedding day, when all may see its golden glow, but for all our tomorrows, until death do us part. Wear it as a sign of my love for you and as a notice to the world that you have chosen me to be your husband/wife."

"_____, with this ring I wed you; with my body I worship you, and with all my worldly goods I endow you."

"As a sign of my commitment and the desire of my heart, I give you this ring. May it always be a reminder that I have chosen you above all other women/men and that, from this day forward, you are my wife/husband."

Minister: "I hold in my hand two beautiful rings, symbolic of a binding contract, to be given and received as bonds of never-ending love and devoted friendship, circles of life and circles of love."

Groom: "With this ring I wed thee and offer it as a symbol of our everlasting love."

Bride: *"With this ring I wed thee and offer it as a symbol of our everlasting love."*

Up close and personal

I'm sure you remember the story of Bill and Kathy, who fell in love at first sight at an engagement party for their mutual friend and were married in the rain and hail. Here are their ring vows:

Minister: *"The perfect circle of a ring symbolizes eternity, while gold is a symbol of all that is pure and holy. As you give these rings to each other, our prayer is that your love for each other will be as eternal and everlasting as these rings. William, place this ring on Kathryn's finger and repeat after me:"*

Bill (repeating after the minister): *"Kathryn, with this ring, I symbolize our union as husband and wife, for today, tomorrow, and all the years to come. Please wear it as a reminder of our deep and abiding love."*

Minister: *"Kathryn, place this ring on William's finger and repeat after me:"*

Kathryn (repeating after the minister): *"William, I also give you this ring as a symbol of our union as husband and wife, for today, tomorrow and all the years to come. Please wear it as a reminder of our deep and abiding love."*

In Morocco, marriages are usually celebrated in the autumn, at the end of the harvest.

"_____, I give you this ring as a symbol, not only of my love for you and my promise to be your faithful husband/wife, but as a reminder that God is also part of our marriage, to be honored and praised every day of our lives."

"_____, whenever the world sees this ring on your finger, it will be a symbol of my love for you. Although I may not be present with you at that moment, I am always faithful to you, honoring you, and cherishing you as my husband/wife."

"This wedding band is a perfect circle of precious metal that symbolizes a man's kingdom and his earthly possessions, and as I place this ring on your finger, I entrust you with my kingdom and possessions. When you look at this ring in the years to come, may it remind you of my vows to you this day and may you always feel encircled by my love, just as this band encircles your finger."

"_____, I give you this ring as a symbol of my love for you. Let it remind you always, as it circles your finger, of my eternal love, surrounding you and enfolding you day and night."

"You are my beloved bride/groom, and I marry you today with this ring as I give you my heart, my body, and the very breath of my soul."

"Just as this gold band wraps endlessly around your finger, so shall my love always wrap around the very breath of your soul. May it be a reminder of the sacred vows I have spoken this day."

Minister (to the bride and groom): *"I will ask you now to seal the vows which you have just made by the giving and receiving of rings. Let us remember that the circle is the emblem of eternity, and it is our prayer that your love and happiness will be as unending as the rings which you exchange."*

Minister (to the groom): *"_____, do you have a token of your love?"*

Groom: *"Yes, a ring. This ring I give thee, in token and pledge, of our constant faith and abiding love."*

Minister (to the bride): *"_____, do you have a token of your love?"*

Bride: *"Yes, a ring. This ring I give thee, in token and pledge, of our constant faith and abiding love."*

Ring vows with the covenant of salt

Minister: *"For centuries, rings have symbolized the sealing of covenants and commitments. This ring is a circle. It symbolizes the continuity of the marriage bond, a marriage for as long as you both shall live."*

Minister (to the groom): *"Do you, _____, give this ring to _____ as a token of your love for her?"*

Groom: *"I do."*

Minister: *"Then, as a ceaseless reminder of this hour and of the vows you have taken, _____, place this ring on the hand of your bride and repeat after me:"*

Groom (repeating after the minister): *"With this ring I thee wed, with loyal love I thee endow, and all my worldly goods with thee I share, in the name of the Father and the Son and the Holy Spirit. Amen."*

Minister: *"This ring has not always been the beautiful gold that we see here today. It came from the ground as rough ore, that ore had to be tried by a refiner fire, to drive away the impurities; now only the precious gold remains. May this ring be a symbol of difficult times. Problems will come in your marriage, but they can be like the refiner fire that drives away the impurities, leaving only the precious gold of your love, a love that shall grow more precious and beautiful as years pass by."*

Minister (to the bride): *"Do you, _____, give this ring to _____ as an expression of your love for him?"*

Bride: *"I do."*

Minister (to the groom): *"Will you, _____, take this ring from _____ as a token of her love for you, and will you wear it as an expression of your love for her?"*

Groom: *"I will."*

> The chanting of the Seven Wedding Blessings takes place at the end of a Jewish ceremony, while the groom and then the bride sip from a cup of wine.

Minister (to the bride): *"Then, as a ceaseless reminder of this hour and of the vows you have taken, _____, place this ring on the hand of your groom and repeat after me:"*

Bride (repeating after the minister): *"With this ring I thee wed. Entreat me not to leave thee or to return from following after thee, for whither thou goest I will go and where thou lodgest I will lodge. Thy people shall be my people and thy God my God."*

Minister (to the bride and groom): *"You have just sealed your covenant by the giving and receiving of rings. The most beautiful example of this partnership is the marriage relationship. You have committed here today to share the rest of your lives with each other and that nothing, save death, will ever cause you to part. You entered this relationship as two distinct individuals, but from this day forth your lives will be so totally melded together that you will never be able to separate.*

"This covenant relationship is symbolized through the pouring of these two individual bags of salt—one representing you, _____, and all that you were, all that you are, and all that you will ever be, and the other representing you, _____, and all that you were, all that you are, and all that you will ever be. As these two bags of salt are poured into the third bag, the individual bags of salt will no longer exist, but will be joined together as one. Just as these grains of salt can never separated and poured again into the individual bags, so will your marriage be. Far more important than your individuality is now the reality that you are no longer two, but one, never to be separated one from the other."

Some traditionalists believe that a bride should wear three rings on her wedding day: one on her finger, a wreath on her head, and a circular brooch over her heart.

146

"_____ and _____, we have heard your vows and you've symbolized your union by pledging your lives to each other, exchanging rings and through the Covenant of Salt. So, by the authority of God's word and the state of _____, as a minister of the Gospel, I now pronounce you husband and wife."

Up close and personal

These are the personalized wedding vows of Eric and Kimberly, whose story you will read about in a later chapter. Here are the personalized ring vows they wrote for their ceremony:

Minister: *"The exchanging of rings has great meaning to Eric and Kimberly. These rings that they have chosen are engraved with a repeating pattern that, like the rings themselves, have no beginning and no end. Neither Kimberly nor Eric can remember when their love began, yet both can say it will have no end. By exchanging rings, Kimberly and Eric can show to each other and to all the love that they share."*

Kimberly (repeating after the minister as she places the ring on Eric's finger): *"Eric, I give you this ring as a sign to you and to all the love I carry only for you. I give it knowing that our love is in constant need of encouragement, yet is a constant in our lives. With patience, understanding, and communication, it will continue to grow. Accept this ring, knowing it comes from my heart and soul. Take it and wear it, that all who see it may know that I love you."*

Eric (repeating after the minister as he places the ring on Kimberly's finger): *"Kimberly, I give you this ring as a sign to you and to all of the love that I carry only for you. I give it, knowing that our love is in constant need of encouragement, yet is a constant in our lives. With patience, understanding, and communication, it* will continue to grow. Accept this ring, knowing that it comes from my heart and soul. Take it and wear it, that all who see it may know that I love you."

Reaffirmation service

"We have lived and loved as we promised long ago in the presence of God, and our past and our future are an unbroken circle, like this ring, with which I renew my pledge to you of never ending devotion."

"With this ring I reaffirm my love for you, a love refined in the crucible of our togetherness. Wear it as my prayer of thanksgiving and of my hopes for all our tomorrows."

"First came the engagement ring, a promise of our wedding yet to come. Then came the gold band I placed on your finger on our wedding day when I promised to love you and cherish you until the end of my days. Now comes this ring of renewal, celebrating our _____ precious years of married life together and the joyous years yet to come. With this ring I reaffirm my love for you."

> European tradition says that the first things a new bride should bring to her new home are a broom, a box of salt, a head of garlic, and a Bible.

$\mathscr{C}$HAPTER NINE

VOWS INSPIRED BY THE CLASSICS

Many couples take phrasings from classical writings and incorporate them into their wedding vows. In this chapter, I have gathered a sampling of some of the more popular selections.

As you read through these selections, keep in mind that you may use one in its entirety, combine it with other writings, or select specific phrases that can be incorporated into your own vows.

Drinking rituals are used in most Chinese weddings. The sharing of the vows is publicly demonstrated by the bride and groom sharing a drink of wine mixed with honey. They drink from two cups tied together with a red silk thread.

Let me not to the marriage of true minds

Admit impediments. Love is not love

Which alters when it alteration finds,

Or bends with the remover to remove:

O, no! It is an ever-fix'd mark,

That looks on tempests and is never shaken;

It is the star to every wandering bark,

Whose worth's unknown, although his height be taken.

Love's not Time's fool, though rosy lips and cheeks

Within his bending sickle's compass come;

Love alters not with his brief hours and weeks,

But bears it out even to the edge of doom.

If this be error and upon me prov'd,

I never writ, nor no man ever lov'd.

William Shakespeare, Sonnet CXVI

Shall I compare thee to a summer's day?

Thou art more lovely and more temperate...

When in eternal lines to time thou grow'st

So long as men can breathe or eyes can see,

So long lives this, and this gives life to thee.

William Shakespeare, Sonnet XVIII

Let those who are in favour with their stars

Of public honour and proud titles boast,

Whilst I, whom fortune of such triumph bars

Unlook'd for joy in that I honour most.

Great princes' favourites their fair leaves spread

But as the marigold at the sun's eye,

And in themselves their pride lies buried,

For at a frown they in their glory die.

The painful warrior famoused for fight,

After a thousand victories once foiled,

Is in the book of honour raged quite,

And all the rest forgot for which he toiled:

Then happy I that love and am beloved

Where I may not remove nor be removed.

William Shakespeare, Sonnet XXV

But here's the joy: my friend and I are one...

Then she loves but me alone!

William Shakespeare, Sonnet KLII

Thy love is better than high birth to me,

Richer than wealth, prouder than garments' cost,

Of more delight than hawks or horses be;

And, having thee, of all men's pride I boast...

William Shakespeare, Sonnet XCI

> *In India, the groom's brother will sprinkle flower petals over the bridal couple at the end of the marriage ceremony.*

151

Love one another, but make not a bond of love:

Let it rather be a moving sea between the shores of your souls.

Fill each other's cup but drink not from one cup.

Give one another of your bread but eat not from the same loaf.

Sing and dance together and be joyous, but let each one of you be alone,

Even as the strings of a lute are alone though they quiver with the same music.

Give your hearts, but not into each other's keeping.

For only the hand of Life can contain your hearts.

And stand together yet not too near together:

For the pillars of the temple stand apart,

And the oak tree and the cypress grow not in each other's shadow.

Kahlil Gibran

"Love gives naught but itself and takes naught but from itself. Love possesses not nor would it be possessed; for love is sufficient unto love."

Kahlil Gibran

"Sensual pleasure passes and vanishes in the twinkling of an eye, but the friendship between us, the mutual confidence, the

152

delights of the heart, the enchantment of the soul, these things do not perish and can never be destroyed. I shall love you until I die."

Voltaire

"It is the man and woman united that makes the complete human being. Separate she lacks his force of body and strength of reason; he her softness, sensibility and acute discernment. Together they are most likely to succeed in the world."

Benjamin Franklin

Orthodox and Conservative Jewish weddings may not be held during the "Three Weeks" between the 17th of Tammuz and the 9th of Av, or during the "Sefirah," the seven weeks between Passover and Shavout.

"There is no more lovely, friendly and charming relationship, communion or company than a good marriage."

Martin Luther

O my Luve's like a red, red rose

That's newly sprung in June;

O my Luve's like the melodie

That's sweetly played in tune.

As fair art thou, my bonnie lass,

153

So deep in luve am I;

And I will luve thee still, my dear,

Till a' the seas gang dry.

Robert Burns

A new idea is to have the groom meet his bride and her father halfway down the aisle. The bride and groom then approach the altar together.

"Marriage is the golden ring in a chain whose beginning is a glance and whose ending is Eternity."

Kahlil Gibran

Tonight is a night of union and also of scattering of the stars,

for a bride is coming from the sky: the full moon.

The sky is an astrolabe, and the Law is Love.

Jalal Al-Din Rumi, Persian Love Poem

Come live with me, and be my love,

And we will some new pleasures prove

Of golden sands, and crystal brooks,

With silken lines, and silver hooks

John Donne

"*To get the full value of joy, you must have someone to divide it with.*"

Mark Twain

"*Better is a heart full of love, than a mind filled with knowledge.*"

Charles Dickens

"*Friendship is a union of spirits, a marriage of hearts, and the bond of virtue.*"

William Penn

"*...and yet even while I was exulting in my solitude I became aware of a strange lack. I wished a companion to lie near me in the starlight, silent and not moving, but ever within touch. For there is a fellowship more quiet even than solitude, and which, rightly understood, is solitude made perfect. And to live...with the woman a man loves is of all lives the most complete and free.*"

Robert Louis Stevenson, from "A Night Among the Pines"

155

Go seek her out all courteously,

And say I come,

Wind of spices whose song is ever

Epithalamium.

O hurry over the dark lands

And run upon the sea

For seas and land shall not divide us

My love and me.

Now, wind, of your good courtesy

I pray you go,

And come into her little garden

And sing at her window;

Singing: The bridal wind is blowing

For Love is at his noon;

And soon will your true love be with you,

Soon, O soon.

James Joyce, Poem XIII

Oh, hasten not this loving act,

Rapture where self and not-self meet;

My life has been the awaiting you,

Your footfall was my own heart's beat.

Paul Valery

When our two souls stand up erect and strong,

Face to face, silent, drawing nigh and nigher,

Until the lengthening wings break into fire

At either curved point,—what bitter wrong

Can the earth do us, that we should not long

Be here contented! Think. In mounting higher,

The angels would press on us and aspire

To drop some golden orb of perfect song

Into our deep, dear silence. Let us stay

Rather on earth, Beloved—where the unfit

contrarious moods of men recoil away

And isolate pure spirits, and permit

A place to stand and love in for a day...

How do I love thee? Let me count the ways.

I love thee to the depth and breadth and height

My soul can reach, when feeling out of sight

> Guests at a Mexican wedding
> gather around the bridal couple and
> form the shape of a heart.

For the ends of Being and ideal Grace.

I love thee to the level of everyday's

Most quiet need, by sun and candle-light.

I love thee freely, as men strive for Right;

I love thee purely, as they turn from Praise.

I love thee with the passion put to use

In my old griefs, and with my childhood's faith.

I love thee with a love I seemed to lose

With my lost saints,—I love thee with the breath,

Smiles, tears, of all my life!—and, if God choose,

I shall but love thee better after death.

Elizabeth Barrett Browning, *Sonnets from the Portuguese*

Vows based on scripture

"And the Lord God caused a deep sleep to fall upon Adam, and he slept: and he took one of his ribs, and closed up the flesh instead thereof; and the rib, which the Lord God had taken from man, made he a woman, and brought her unto the man. And Adam said, This is now bone of my bones, and flesh of my flesh: she shall be called Woman, because she was taken out of Man. Therefore shall a man leave his father and his mother and shall cleave unto his wife: and they shall be one flesh. And so, just as Eve was

In Jewish tradition it is customary to have a cantor chant the benedictions instead of having them read by the rabbi.

formed from Adam's rib, not from his head as to rule him, or from his foot to be stepped on, but from his side, to be a helpmate, a partner in life, you have been given to me by God, _____, to be my partner as we walk side by side through life together and I hereby vow before God and these witnesses to be a true and faithful husband to you, always nurturing, comforting and supporting, loving you until I live no more."

Genesis 2:21–24

"But from the beginning of the creation God made them male and female. For this cause shall a man leave his father and mother, and cleave to his wife; and they twain shall be one flesh: so then they are no more twain, but one flesh. What therefore God hath joined together, let not man put asunder. _____, as we are united in marriage this day, we shall also cleave to each other, no longer twain, but becoming one flesh, and no forces on earth can ever tear us apart. I pledge my love to you eternally until death parts us."

Mark 10:6–9

"Two are better than one; because they have a good reward for their labour. For if they fall, the one will lift up his fellow; but woe to him that is alone when he falleth; for he hath not another to help him up. Again, if two lie together, then they have heat; but how can one be warm alone? And if one prevail against him, two shall withstand him; and a threefold cord is not quickly broken."

"_____, I promise, as the scripture says, to stand by your side, always ready to help you up; I promise to lie by your side, always ready to warm you; and I promise to prevail with you, always ready to withstand the hardships of this world. Our marriage bond will be strong, unbreakable, eternal, and I pledge this to you before these witnesses, so help me God."

Ecclesiastes 4:9–12

"Entreat me not to leave thee,

Or to return from following after thee:

For wither thou goest, I will go,

And where thou lodgest, I will lodge.

Thy people shall be my people,

And thy God my God.

Where thou diest, will I die,

And there will I be buried.

The Lord do so to me, and more also,

If ought but death part thee and me."

Ruth 1:16–17

An Episcopal minister must obtain the consent of a bishop before officiating at a second marriage that includes a divorced person.

"So ought men to love their wives as their own bodies. He that loveth his wife loveth himself. For no man ever yet hated his own flesh; but nourisheth and cherisheth it, even as the Lord the church: For we are members of his body, of his flesh, and of his bones. For this cause shall a man leave his father and mother, and shall be joined unto his wife, and the two shall become one flesh. This is a great mystery: but I speak concerning Christ and the church. Nevertheless let every one of you in particular so love his wife even as himself; and the wife see that she reverence her husband."

Ephesians 5:28–33

"My beloved spake, and said unto me, Rise up, my love, my fair one, and come away. For, lo, the winter is past, the rain is over and gone. The flowers appear on the earth; the time of the singing of birds is come, and the voice of the turtle is heard in our land. The fig tree putteth forth her green figs, and the vines with the tender grape give a good smell. Arise, my love, my fair one, and come away. O my dove, that art in the clefts of the rock, in the secret places of the stairs, let me see thy countenance, let me hear thy voice; for sweet is thy voice, and thy countenance is comely. Take us the foxes, the little foxes, that spoil the vines; for our vines have tender grapes. My beloved is mine, and I am his: he feedeth among the lilies. Until the day break, and the shadows flee away, turn, my beloved, and be thou like a roe or a young hart upon the mountains of Bether."

Song of Solomon 2:10–17

Here are other portions of scripture you may wish to consider:

Hebrews 13:4	Matthew 22:35–40
Matthew 19:4–6	Romans 12:1–2, 9–18
John 2:1–11	Colossians 3:12–13
I John 4:7–19	Proverbs 3:3–6
I Peter 3:7	Ephesians 4:1–4, 5:12

Song of Solomon 7:11–12, 8:6b–7
Isaiah 43:1–5, 54:10, 60:19–22

Native American verses

"Now we feel no rain, for each of us will be shelter to the other. Now we will feel no cold, for each of us will be warmth to the other. Now there is no loneliness for us. Now we are two bodies, but only one life. We go now to our dwelling place, to enter into the days of our togetherness. May our days be good and long upon this earth."

Apache Indian prayer

Fair is the white star of twilight, and the sky clearer at the day's end; but she is fairer, and she is dearer, She, my heart's friend.

Fair is the white star of twilight, and the moon roving to the sky's end; but she is fairer, better worth loving, She, my heart's friend.

Shoshone Indian poem

> In the Middle Ages, the giving of a simple gold wedding ring constituted a legal marriage, even if no one else was there to witness it.

Oh, I am thinking

Oh, I am thinking

I have found my lover.

Oh, I think it is so.

Chippewa Indian poem of betrothal

I know not whether thou has been absent:

I lie down with thee, I rise up with thee,

In my dreams thou art with me.

If my eardrops tremble in my ears,

I know it is thou moving within my heart.

Aztec wedding poem

"O Morning Star! When you look down upon us, give us peace and refreshing sleep. Great Spirit! Bless our children, friends, and visitors through a happy life. May our trails lie straight and level before us. Let us live to be old. We are all your children and ask these things with good hearts."

Traditional wedding prayer of the Great Plains Indian

"You are my husband/wife

My feet shall run because of you.

My feet, dance because of you.

My eyes, see because of you.

My mind, think because of you.

And I shall love because of you."

Old Eskimo Indian wedding vow

Classical vows for the reaffirmation service

If you are planning a formal reaffirmation service, you may wish to incorporate classical writings into your reaffirmation vows, drawing from Elizabeth Barrett Browning's letters, for example, or from the Bible or Shakespeare's many writings. Shakespeare's sonnets work especially well, in fact, and here are several of them that may be used in their entirety, if so desired. You and your spouse may alternate lines, if you wish, or you may each recite your own sonnet.

Shall I compare thee to a summer's day?

Thou art more lovely and more temperate.

Rough winds do shake the darling buds of May,

And summer's lease hath all too short a date.

And often is his gold complexion dimmed;

And every fair from fair sometime declines,

By chance or nature's changing course untrimmed.

But thy eternal summer shall not fade,

Nor lose possession of that fair thou ow'st,

Nor shall Death brag thou wand'rest in his shade,

When in eternal lines to time thou grow'st.

So long as men can breathe or eyes can see,

So long lives this, and this gives life to thee.

William Shakespeare, Sonnet XVIII

Devouring Time, blunt thou the lion's paws,

And make the earth devour her own sweet brood;

Pluck the keen teeth from the fierce tiger's jaws,

And burn the long-lived phoenix in her blood;

Make glad and sorry seasons as thou fleet'st,

And do whate'er thou wilt, swift-footed Time,

To the wide world and all her fading sweets.

But I forbid thee one most heinous crime:

O, carve not with thy hours my love's fair brow,

Nor draw no lines there with thine antique pen;

Him in thy course untainted do allow

For beauty's pattern to succeeding men.

Yet do thy worst, Old Time; despite thy wrong,

My love shall in my verse ever live young.

William Shakespeare, Sonnet XIX

To me, fair friend, you never can be old,

For as you were when first your eye I eyed,

Such seems your beauty still. Three winters cold

Have from the forests shook three summers' pride,

Three beauteous springs to yellow autumn turned

In process of the seasons have I seen,

Three April perfumes in three hot Junes burned,

Since first I saw you fresh, which yet are green.

Ah, yet doth beauty, like a dial hand,

Steal from his figure, and no pace perceived;

So your sweet hue, which methinks still doth stand,

Hath motion, and mine eye may be deceived;

For fear of which, hear this, thou age unbred:

Ere you were born was beauty's summer dead.

William Shakespeare, Sonnet CIV

Those lines that I before have writ do lie,

Even those that said I could not love you dearer.

Yet then my judgement knew no reason why

My most full flame should afterwards burn clearer.

But reckoning Time, whose millioned accidents

Creep in 'twixt vows and change decrees of kings,

Tan sacred beauty, blunt the sharp'st intents,

Divert strong minds to th' course of alt'ring things—

Alas, why, fearing of Time's tyranny,

Might I not then say 'Now I love you best,'

When I was certain o'er incertainty,

Crowning the present, doubting of the rest?

Love is a babe; then might I not say so,

To give full growth to that which still doth grow.

William Shakespeare, Sonnet CXV

Shakespeare wrote 154 sonnets, all of which are available in a single volume at your local library. You will enjoy perusing through them, perhaps selecting a line or phrase here and there. Be sure to read Sonnets 15, 25, 76, 88, and 91, all of which offer lovely phrasings for your consideration. They may even inspire you to wax eloquent and compose an original sonnet of your very own!

> *A Welsh bride's bouquet is often laid on the grave of a parent or grandparent, as a sign of respect for those who are unable to be present on the wedding day.*

Like as the waves make toward pebbled shore,

So do our minutes hasten to their end,

Each changing place with that which goes before,

In sequent toil all forwards do content.

Nativity, once in the main of light,

Crawls to maturity, wherewith, being crowned,

Crooked eclipses 'gainst his glory fight

And Time that gave, doth now his gift confound.

Time doth transfix the flourish set on youth,

And delves the parallels in beauty's brow,

Feeds on the rarities of natures truth,

And nothing stands but for his scythe to mow;

And yet, to times, in hope, my verse shall stand,

Praising thy worth, despite his cruel hand.

William Shakespeare, Sonnet LX

Thy bosom is endeared with all hearts,

Which I by lacking have supposed dead;

And there reigns Love, and all Love's loving parts,

And all those friends which I thought buried.

How many a holy and obsequious tear

Hath dear religious love stol'n from mine eye,

As interest of the dead, which now appear

But things remov'd that hidden in thee lie!

Thou art the grave where buried love doth live,

Hung with the trophies of my lovers gone,

Who all their parts of me to thee did give,

That due of many now is thine alone:

Their images I lov'd, I view in thee,

And thou (all they) hast all the all of me.

William Shakespeare, Sonnet XXXI

Sweet love, renew thy force; be it not said

Thy edge should blunter be than appetite,

Which but to-day by feeding is allay'd,

To-morrow sharpened in his former might:

So, love, be thou, although to-day thou fill

Thy hungry eyes, even till they wink with fulness,

To-morrow see again, and do not kill

The spirit of love, with a perpetual dulness.

Let this sad interim like the ocean be

Which parts the shore, where two contracted new

Come daily to the banks, that when they see

Return of love, more blest may be the view;

As call it winter, which being full of care,

Makes summer's welcome, thrice more wished, more rare.

William Shakespeare, Sonnet LVI

Let not my love be called idolatry,

Nor my beloved as an idol show,

Since all alike my songs and praises be

To one, of one, still such, and ever so.

Kind is my love to-day, to-morrow kind,

Still constant in a wondrous excellence;

Therefore my verse to constancy confined,

One thing expressing, leaves out difference.

Fair, kind, and true, is all my argument,

Fair, kind, and true, varying to other words;

And in this change is my invention spent,

Three themes in one, which wondrous scope affords.

Fair, kind, and true, have often lived alone,

Which three till now, never kept seat in one.

William Shakespeare, Sonnet CV

Another source of inspiration are the writings of Kahlil Gibran, including his love letters to Mary Haskell, the great love of his life. Here are excerpts from some of these letters that will work well for your affirmation vows:

> It is a German tradition for the friends of the bride and groom to come to the bride's home the evening before the wedding to break dishes on her doorstep.

"The most wonderful thing, Mary, is that you and I are always walking together, hand in hand, in a strangely beautiful world, unknown to other people. Love says, you are myself."

"You have the great gift of understanding, beloved Mary. You are a life-giver, Mary. My knowing you is the greatest thing in my days and nights, a miracle. That which is between us is like the Absolute in Life—everchanging, evergrowing. You and I, Mary, understand each other's larger self: and that to me is the most wonderful thing in life."

"Sometimes you have not even begun to speak—and I am at the end of what you are saying."

"I am so happy in your happiness. To you happiness is a form of freedom, and of all the people I know you should be the freest. Surely you have earned this happiness and this freedom. Life cannot be but kind and sweet to you. You have been so sweet and kind to life."

"Marriage doesn't give one any rights in another person except such rights that a person gives—nor any freedom except the freedom which that person gives."

"That deepest thing, that recognition, that knowledge, that sense of kinship began the first time I saw you, and it is the same now - only a thousand times deeper and tenderer. I shall love you to eternity. I loved you long before we met in this flesh. I knew that when I first saw you. It was destiny. We are together like this and nothing can shake us apart."

> An old Irish saying warns that if you marry during the harvest season, you'll never have rest from work and worry.

"Mary, you are the only person in the world with whom I feel wholly at home. The bond between you and me is greater than either of us knows. Between us the bond can't be broken. May Life sing in your heart, and may Life keep you in her most sacred heart."

"I shall love you to eternity. I loved you long before we met in this flesh. I knew that when I first saw you. It was destiny...nothing can shake us apart...I can't and God himself can't."

"The relation between you and me is the most beautiful thing in my life: It is eternal. Mary, I am always asking much of you, and like life itself you always give much. May God bless you for all that you do for me...may God love you and keep you near His heart."

The writings of John Keats offers beautiful phrasings for reaffirmation vows, including these:

"July 1, 1819

...for myself I know not how to express my devotion to so fair a form: I want a brighter word than bright, a fairer word than fair. I almost wish we were butterflies and liv'd but three summer days— three such days with you I could fill with more delight than fifty common years could ever contain..."

"March 1820

...my dear Girl I love you ever and ever and without reserve. The more I have known you the more have I lov'd. In every way— even my jealousies have been agonies of Love, in the hottest fit I ever had I would have died for you. I have vex'd you too much.

But for Love! Can I help it? You are always new. The last of your kisses was ever the sweetest; the last smile the brightest; the last movement the gracefullest...no ill prospect has been able to turn your thoughts a moment from me...even if you did not love me I could not help an entire devotion to you: how much more deeply then must I feel for you knowing you love me..."

Grow old along with me!

The best is yet to be,

The last of life, for which the first was made:

Our times are in his hand

Who saith, "A whole I planned,

Youth shows but half; trust God: see all, nor be afraid!"...

Robert Browning, from Rabbi Ben Ezra

A thing of beauty is a joy forever:

Its loveliness increases; it will never

Pass into nothingness; but still will keep

A bower quiet for us, and a sleep

Full of sweet dreams...

John Keats, Sonnet XIV

If thou must love me, let it be for nought

Except for love's sake only. Do not say,

'I love her for her smile—her look—her way

Of speaking gently,—for a trick of thought

That falls in well with mine, and certes brought

A sense of pleasant ease on such a day'—

For these things in themselves, Beloved, may

Be changed, or change for thee,—and love, so wrought,

May be unwrought so. Neither love me for

Thine own dear pity's wiping my cheeks dry,—

A creature might forget to weep, who bore

Thy comfort long, and lose thy love thereby!

But love me for love's sake, that evermore

Thou mayest love on, through love's eternity.

Elizabeth Barrett Browning, from *Sonnets from the Portuguese*

...I give you my hand!

I give you my love more precious than money,

I give you myself before preaching or law;

Will you give me yourself? will you come travel with me?

Shall we stick by each other as long as we live?

Walt Whitman, from *Song of the Open Road*

If ever two were one, then surely we.

If ever man were lov'd by wife, then thee;

If ever wife was happy in a man,

Compare with me ye women if you can.

I prize thy love more than whole Mines of gold,

Or all the riches that the East doth hold.

My love is such that Rivers cannot quench,

Nor ought but love from thee, give recompence.

Thy love is such I can no way repay,

The heavens reward thee manifold I pray.

Then while we live, in love let's so persever,

That when we live no more, we may live ever.

Anne Bradstreet, *To My Dear and Loving Husband*

> *Pennsylvania Dutch brides are tossed over a broom by the unmarried women at the wedding reception*

CHAPTER TEN
THEME WEDDING VOWS

The 21st century has brought us an array of theme weddings, which require special wedding vows that are appropriate to each theme. First, we have holiday weddings, which can occur on such days as Valentine's Day or Christmas Day. Then come nature weddings that take place outdoors, whether in a garden or along the seashore. After that we have the period weddings, which have gained in popularity over the past decade. Period weddings usually have a Renaissance or Victorian theme, though you can certainly develop a theme that suits you and your beloved. Finally, we discover the poignant covenant wedding.

> *It was an early Roman custom for a married couple to drink wine made of honey for a month after their marriage. A month was then known as a "moon." This time became known as the "month of honey" or "honey moon."*

Valentine's Day ceremony

"It is fitting that we marry on Valentine's Day, the most romantic day of the year, when lovers celebrate their love. Truly, we celebrate our love today as our hearts are joined in holy, sacred

matrimony. I will hold gently the heart you have given me this day, a lasting treasure to be cherished, and I give my heart to you with joy and abandonment, as I promise to be your faithful husband/wife. Every year we will reaffirm our vows on Valentine's Day, as we celebrate our wedding day, the day we gave our hearts to each other until the end of time."

"I give my heart to you completely as your husband/wife; from this moment on, it will always be with you. There will be no escape from my love. If you fly away, I will fly after you. If you walk down a secret path, I will follow you. If you sail away to the farthest corner of the earth, I will find you, because you are mine; you belong to me. And if you should fall, I will lift you up. If you should feel weak, I will cover you with my strength. From this day forward, you are in my heart and I am in yours. Our hearts are intertwined and will beat as one. Nothing will ever separate us."

Let me not to the marriage of true minds
Admit impediments. Love is not love
Which alters when it alteration finds,
Or bends with the remover to remove:
O, no! it is an ever-fixed mark,
That looks on tempests and is never shaken;
It is the star to every wandering bark,
Whose worth's unknown, although his height be taken.
Love's not Time's fool, though rosy lips and cheeks
Within his bending sickle's compass come;
Love alters not with his brief hours and weeks,

But bears it out even to the edge of doom.
If this be error and upon me proved,
I never writ, nor no man ever loved.

William Shakespeare, Sonnet CXVI

New Year's Day ceremony

"As we put the past behind us and embark on a new year, so we put our individual lives behind us as we become one in holy matrimony. And just as a new year is bright and promising, so you are my new day, my hope, my joy and the sunshine of our future together. Take my hand and walk with me into the new year and into our new life as my husband/wife. I give you my heart and everything that I am as we begin our lives together."

"Today is a new beginning, a new year and a new life together as husband and wife. I take you this day as my husband/wife. I promise to love you in good times and bad, in plenty and in want, in sickness and in health, for all the new years to come."

Christmas Day ceremony

"Christmas is the birthday of Jesus Christ, God's sacrificial gift to us, and so we have come to marry on this sacred day and give ourselves to each other in the spirit of Christmas, with a holy, sacrificial love for each other. On this silent night/sacred day, I give myself to you, _____, as your loving, faithful husband/wife, as I offer my gift of love to you, a gift that shall endure until the end of time. Every year of our lives, as we gather during the

Christmas season and give gifts to each other, I promise to give myself anew to you in remembrance and honor of the vows we are taking here today."

Groom: "_____, *this is a holy, sacred season that has deep meaning for both of us. It is a season of love and of giving. What better time than this for us to marry? You are the best Christmas present I've ever received, and I take you as my wife this day. I promise to love you and to be faithful to you as long as we both shall live."*

Bride: "_____, *and you are my precious gift. I take you today as my husband. I promise to love you and honor you as long as we both shall live. When we celebrate our anniversary each year on this date, it will always have special meaning as we remember this day when we gave ourselves as gifts to each other."*

> Navajo Indian brides traditionally marry while facing east, in the direction of the rising sun.

Nature theme weddings

Outdoor weddings have become quite popular for couples who want to escape the confines of a church, or any other manmade edifice. An outdoor wedding evokes a natural ambience, where the bride and groom can enjoy nature's majesty. The following are several appropriate vows for nature weddings.

"As we stand in the shade of God's creation, I offer myself to you as your husband/wife. Our love is reflected in the flower's blooms and the strength of the towering trees, always growing, always searching for perfection, just as the trees reach for the heavens and the blooms open their faces to the sun. Just as this garden/forest is a living thing, so may our union continue always to thrive until death parts us."

❖❖❖

"As we stand in this garden among these exquisite flowers, I offer you the flower of my heart as my wedding gift to you. This flower is pure and innocent, beautiful and eternal. It needs the care and nourishment that only you can give it. Place this flower within your own heart. Love it, keep it safe, give it light, and may it bloom forever from this day forward, as I commit it to you with my eternal love as your wife/husband."

❖❖❖

"_____, I give myself to you this day, to be your husband/wife. I promise to love you with a love as pure and lovely as the snow, and a heart as warm as the radiant sun overhead. I promise to be true to you all the days of my life, with a loyalty and devotion as immense and seamless as the sky above."

❖❖❖

Groom: "_____, as we stand here in this magnificent setting, I vow to love you and be true to you as long as we both shall live. And as the trees stand tall and provide safety and shelter against the storm, I promise to provide for you and be your shelter for any storms we may face together."

Bride: "_____, I vow to love you and be true to you for as long as we both shall live. Just as these mountains are strong and enduring, so my love will always be for you."

"As we stand beside the ocean tide, may our love always be as constant and unchanging as these waves that wash beneath our feet, flowing endlessly from the depths of the sea. Your love came softly upon my heart, just as the foam comes softly upon the sand. And just as there will never be a morning without the ocean's flow, so there will never be a day without my love for you. I pledge myself to you this day and I promise to be your faithful husband/wife, as unchanging and dependable as the tide; as these waters nourish the earth and sustain life, may my constant love nourish and sustain you until the end of time."

Groom: "_____, as we stand in this glorious place, surrounded by our friends and family, I take you to be my wife. I promise to love you with a love as deep and wide as this ocean, and I promise to stand beside you through good times and bad, through plenty and want, through sickness and health, as steady and dependable as these unceasing waves crashing against the sand."

Bride: "_____, I take you to be my husband. I promise to love you with a love so immense and boundless that it can't be measured, just as no one can count the grains of sand on this beach. I promise to stand beside you through good times and bad, through plenty and want, through sickness and health, as sure and steady as the flight of the seagulls soaring overhead."

"As the sea is eternal, so is our love. As the wind is all-encompassing, so is our love. As the earth is solid beneath our feet, so is our love. And yet, our love is so great that it even soars beyond the sea and the wind and the earth. It is so perfect to be standing beside you here, among these elements which reflect the love we have for each other. Every year on our anniversary, we will come here, to stand on this very spot, as we commit ourselves to each other anew, just as I commit myself to you this day."

Up close and personal

This is the story of Eric and Kimberly, who met at a country western dance bar by the name of Cactus Jack's. The night they met, Kimberly bravely invited him to go to the movies with her and a few friends. The sparks flew, and as Kimberly says, their relationship "just fell into place." Within two weeks they "knew it was forever," and they are now engaged to be married.

Their outdoor wedding will have a country western theme with the men wearing black jeans, black boots, cowboy hats, and country-cut vests with prairie ties. Kimberly's wedding gown is being created by her grandmother from a pattern they found in the Harper House Past Patterns catalog. She's going to wear white boots, a floral tiara, and her hair in a Gibson Girl bun. The judge who will marry them has agreed to wear traditional parson's attire.

Eric and Kimberly have written their own vows for their wedding and have graciously agreed to share them. The vows will be integrated with a Unity Candle ceremony.

Eric (to Kimberly) and Kimberly (to Eric): "I, Kimberly/Eric, take you, Eric/Kimberly, to be my lawfully wedded husband/wife. I promise before our families, friends, and the Lord, to care for you in sickness and in sadness, and I promise to laugh with you and rejoice with you in gladness. I promise to inspire greatness in you and to listen and give to you from my heart and soul. I make this vow in love, keep it in faith, live it in hope, and share it in honesty, as long as our souls shall live."

These vows will be followed by the Unity Candle Ceremony, which consists of the lighting of a central candle from two separate candles held by the bride and groom to symbolize the uniting of two lives into one. Their wedding vows will be inscribed on the large unity candle. In the years to come, on each wedding anniversary, they will reaffirm these vows as they again light the candle in celebration. Kim and Eric have also composed beautifully worded ring vows; look for them in Chapter Eight.

Period weddings

The past 15 years has seen an increasing interest in Celtic, Renaissance, and Victorian theme weddings. This fervor has been spurred by the touching Celtic vows in the movie *Braveheart*, as well as the burgeoning popularity of Renaissance festivals.

Celtic ceremony

A Celtic marriage ceremony is pure and simple. In Braveheart, the bride and groom met in the quiet and privacy of the forest to pledge their vows and have their marriage sanctified and blessed. The groom brought a piece of his family plaid to the ceremony, which he gave to the priest, who wrapped it around the couple's wrists as the couple exchanged these simple words of commitment:

Groom: *"I will love you my whole life and no other."*

Young Amish boys playfully toss the groom over a low fence to symbolize his passage into a new life as a married man.

Bride: *"And I you, and no other."*

Many modern couples create their own Celtic vows, incorporating poetic phrases from *Anam Cara*, a book written by John O'Donohue. O'Donohue is described as a "poet, philosopher, and scholar who guides you through the spiritual landscape of the Irish imagination. In Anam Cara, Gaelic for 'soul friend,' the ancient teachings, stories, and blessings of Celtic wisdom provide. . . profound insights on the universal themes of friendship . . .and love . . ." (See the Bibliography at the back of this book.)

Renaissance ceremony

The Renaissance age is the period when Christopher Columbus set sail and Henry VIII reigned in England. Renaissance festivals are extremely popular today, and depict an age of chivalry when a Lady presented her Knight with her favor to wear on his sleeve when he went into a battle or a joust.

Groom: *"I taketh thy hand in mine, my lady, my truest love, and looketh upon thy gracious countenance, as I pledge mine oath and troth to thee in vow of matrimony. I forsake mine ancient ways, and all others from mine past, to cleave unto thee, for all eternities to come, as thy devoted husband. Before these goode witnesses, I giveth myself to thee this day, to be thy protectorate and thy sustainer throughout all our lives. From this day forth, may we be not two, but one. I loveth thee, my Lady _____."*

Bride: *"I accept thy pledge, my Lord, my love, and I also pledge mine oath and troth to thee in vow of matrimony. I shall loveth thee and careth for thee all the days of our lives. Before these goode witnesses, I giveth myself to thee this day, to joineth with thee as we be not two, but one, for all eternity. I loveth thee, mine Lord _____."*

The marriage and ring vows may be read from a parchment scroll on which the vows have been written with a black calligraphy pen. After the ceremony, this scroll may be framed as a memento of the wedding.

Groom: *"My dearest Lady wife, _____, this ring doth represent my never-ending love for thee for all eternities to come. May it beareth witness to all who behold this golden circlet on thy finger that we two be bonded in sacred matrimony."*

Bride: *"I thank thee, _____, for thy most valued golden circlet representing thy love. I now placeth on thine finger a symbol of mine love and vow, as witness to all that I and thee be bonded in sacred matrimony."*

Victorian ceremony

The Victorian age relates to the period when Queen Victoria reigned in Britain. In today's world of weddings, a Victorian wedding signifies old-fashioned romance. When she married Duke Albert, Queen Victoria wore a dress of white satin, with a crown of orange blossoms. Both of those choices have since become popular traditions in wedding attire. The white dress symbolizes modesty and maidenhood, and the orange blossoms represent fruitfulness.

Groom: "*O my Luve's like a red, red rose, that's newly sprung in June; O my Luve's like the melodie that's sweetly played in tune, as fair as thou, my bonnie lass, so deep in luve am I, and I will luve thee still, my dear, Till a'the seas gang dry. I love you* _____, *and I vow to be true and faithful to you 'til death do us part.*"

Bride: "*O my Luve's like a red, red rose, that's newly sprung in June; O my Luve's like the melodie that's sweetly played in tune, as fair as thou, my handsome lad, so deep in luve am I, and I will luve thee still, my dear, Till a'the seas gang dry. I love you* _____, *and I vow to be true and faithful to you until death do us part.*"

Groom: "*You are my lovely bride, my fair lady. In fact, you are the fairest of all women, and I choose you this day to be my wife. I promise to love you, and to care for you with joy, as a delicate flower. I shan't neglect you, causing you to wilt. But I shall always nourish you with my love, building you up, and encouraging you to bloom evermore with blooms lovelier every year.* _____, *I vow to be true to you and to cherish you every day of my life.*"

Bride: "*You are my handsome groom, a good, upright man. I choose you this day to be my husband. I promise to be your dependable helpmate and to love you and care for you every day for the rest of my life. I shall be your shade, your sanctuary, at the end of each day. I shall always nourish you with my love, building you up, and encouraging you.* _____, *I vow to be true to you and to cherish you every day of my life.*"

Covenant ceremonies

A covenant ceremony is a poignant bonding observance that can be incorporated into any kind of wedding, regardless of its theme. The bonding may take place between the couple and their guests or family members, or only between the bride and groom.

Rose covenant ceremony

A rose ceremony can take place at any wedding venue, whether indoors or outdoors, but it is especially poignant for an outdoor rose garden ceremony. This ceremony usually follows the recitation of the couple's formal wedding vows.

Officiant: "_____ and _____ will now participate in the Ceremony of the Rose. _____(groom) holds a long-stemmed rose that he will present to _____ (bride) and, likewise, _____ (bride) holds a long-stemmed rose that she will present to _____(groom). The water in this vase symbolizes the protection and nourishment their marriage will provide to each other."

Groom (as he hands his bride a long-stemmed white rose): "_____, take this rose as a symbol of my love. It began as a tiny bud and blossomed, just as my love has grown and blossomed for you."

British tradition says that if you start the wedding march with your right foot, you will have good luck in your marriage.

Bride (as she places the rose into a bud vase filled with water): *"I take this rose, a symbol of your love, and I place it into water, a symbol of life. For, just as this rose cannot survive without water, I cannot survive without you."*

Groom: *"In remembrance of this day, I will give you a white rose each year on our anniversary, as a reaffirmation of my love and the vows spoken here today."*

Bride: *"And I will refill this vase with water each year, ready to receive your gift, in reaffirmation of the new life you have given me and the vows spoken here today."*

Groom: *"And so, this rose will be a symbolic memory of my commitment to you this hour. I vow to be a faithful husband to you, to comfort you, honor you, respect you, and cherish you all the days of my life."*

Bride: *"And I commit myself to you, to be a faithful wife, to comfort you, honor you, respect you, and cherish you all the days of my life."*

Handfasting covenant ceremony

Many of today's ceremonies include handfasting as part of the marriage vows, regardless of the type of ceremony. Handfasting, also called "hand tying" or "tying the knot," is often thought of as a Celtic wedding tradition.

The bride's right wrist is tied to the groom's left wrist during the ceremony. This is symbolic of the couple's commitment and devotion to each other. It is popularly believed to be the origin of the phrase "Tying the Knot." Once the bride's and groom's wrists are tied together, the deed is recognized as a binding contract between them and their lives become intertwined for all eternity. In fact, the act of handfasting becomes symbolic of the vows they have taken and their desire to become one. Traditionally, a silk cord has been used for the handfasting; however, many variations have evolved, including the use of different materials and the way the tying takes place.

A rope is used in many Mexican and Latino ceremonies and is draped in a figure eight over the bride's and groom's shoulders. The draping may be performed by the officiant or by a family member. The draping may also be performed by the couple's godmothers, using a rope with a cross to wrap around the couple's shoulders as the couple kneels at the altar.

In an African-American handfasting ceremony, the couple's hands may be tied together using a strip of Kente cloth, a length of braided grass, or a string of cowrie shells. The couple's hands may be tied by the officiant, a family member, or a close friend.

A simple string is used to tie the couple's hands together during a Hindu wedding ceremony in a ritual known as "Hasthagranthi."

The bridal couple may include a handfasting ceremony in their Buddhist marriage service. The fabric or rosary (known as the "mala") is gently tied around the wrists of the bride and groom. The tying may be performed by the officiant or by the parents of the couple.

A Christian couple may use the bride's prayer stole to tie their wrists together, as a symbol of their unity as a married couple and also of their united faith in God. After the officiant has tied their wrists together with the stole, he or she may also bless their union with the sign of the cross.

Sample wording for a handfasting ceremony:

Officiant: "_____ and _____ *have come here today to pledge their vows of marriage.*"

Officiant: "_____, *do you take* _____ *to be your wife? Do you promise to love her, provide for her, and be faithful to her as long as you both shall live?*"

Groom: "*I do.*"

Officiant: "_____, *do you take* _____ *to be your husband? Do you promise to love him, honor him, and be faithful to him as long as you both shall live?*"

Bride: "*I do.*"

Officiant: "_____ and _____, *present your wrists for the handfasting ceremony. As your wrists are fasted together by this cord, you become bound to each other and to the vows you have promised.*"

Commitment by guests or family members

A popular trend is to invite the wedding guests to make a commitment to the bride and groom during the recitation of their wedding vows. This type of ceremony is especially meaningful for a small wedding attended by the bride and groom's closest friends and family members.

This is typical vow wording for this type of ceremony:

Officiant: "_____, *are you ready to make the commitment of marriage to* _____*?*"

Groom: "*Yes, I am.*"

Officiant: "_____, *are you ready to make the commitment of marriage to* _____*?*"

Bride: "*Yes, I am.*"

Officiant addresses the wedding guests: "*Will everyone please stand as we witness* _____ *and* _____ *recite their vows?*"

Groom (repeating after officiant): "*I,* _____*, take you,* _____*, to be my wife, and I promise before God and these witnesses to love you, cherish you, and to keep you special, in plenty and in want, in joy and in sorrow, in sickness and in health, as long as we both shall live.*"

Bride (repeating after officiant): "*I,* _____*take you,* _____*, to be my husband, and I promise before God and these witnesses to love you, cherish you, and to keep you special, in plenty and in want, in joy and in sorrow, in sickness and in health, as long as we both shall.*"

Officiant (to the wedding guests): "*Having witnessed* _____ *and* _____ *recite their wedding vows, will each of you do everything in your power to uphold this couple in their marriage?*"

Guests: "*We do.*"

Jumping the broom ceremony

This is a meaningful African–American tradition dating back to the 17th century. By jumping over the broom at the end of the ceremony, the bride and groom are symbolizing their love and commitment to each other as they establish a new beginning and a home of their own. It's common to decorate the broom with flowers and ribbons. The broom is placed on the floor behind the couple during the marriage ceremony, parallel to the altar (between the couple and the guests).

The bride and groom may recite vows of their own choice, but after being pronounced man and wife, they hold hands and "jump" over the broom.

Ceremony of the wishing stones

A wishing stones ceremony, also known as a blessing stones ceremony, may be incorporated into any type of marriage service. There are many variations of this ceremony, but they each have the same purpose, casting a good wish or a blessing upon the couple during or after the ceremony.

Stones and note cards are given to each guest as they arrive at the ceremony site. The guests are told that the purpose of these stones and note cards will be explained during the wedding service. During the wedding, the officiant explains the meaning of the wishing stones (or blessing stones) and the personal wishes or blessings each guest is asked to describe on the note cards.

Finnish weddings have traditionally been held in the midsummer, because of an association with fertility.

193

The stones may be any attractive stones, from polished agate to river rock. If the wedding is being held outdoors, in a forested area, by a lake or a river, the guests may be asked to gather their own stones from the site.

Once each guest has a stone in hand, he or she is asked to write a personalized wedding wish or blessing for the couple on the card. The cards may be pre-printed with "helper introductions," such as, "My wish for Jim and Sandy is that _____," or "I hope that Jim and Sandy's marriage may be blessed with _____." Alternatively, you can simply provide a blank notecard on which the guests may write their own simple wishes or blessings for the happy couple.

The guests may be asked to read their blessings, or wishes, for the couple as part of the ceremony, or during the wedding reception to follow. In either case, as the guests read off their note cards, they toss their stones into a water-filled container that has been provided for this purpose, placing their note cards in a decorative basket.

The water-filled container may be anything from an elaborate indoor fountain, to a wishing well or a clear glass bowl. The container can become a cherished possession for the newlyweds to display in a prominent place in their home. The note cards are often kept and later integrated into a wedding scrapbook or photo album.

If the ceremony takes place next to a body of water, one variation of this ceremony is for each guest to throw his or her stone into the ocean, lake, or river as each recites his or her wish or blessing for the couple.

Another variation works well for an ocean beach ceremony where, instead of stones, each guest is asked to find a beautiful seashell. The shells are then placed in a container as each guest recites a wish or blessing.

Covenant of salt or sand

This ceremony can be performed using salt or sand. If the wedding is taking place on a sandy beach, it's especially meaningful to perform this ceremony using local sand. Or if both couples are from beach areas, it can be meaningful for each to bring sand from their homes.

The bride and groom each hold a container of salt or sand. The contents of these containers represent their individual lives, with all they were, all they are, and all they will ever be. The bride and groom willingly empty their individual containers of salt or sand into a larger container, symbolizing the joining of their lives for eternity. Just as the grains of salt or sand can never be separated and returned to their individual containers, so the couple is now no longer two, but one, never to be separated one from the other.

The new container of sand can become a touching keepsake for the bride and groom. It is a physical reminder of the joining of two souls in matrimony.

> *In Poland, a bride usually wears an embroidered apron over her wedding gown. Guests discreetly tuck money into its pockets while dancing with her during the "apron dance."*

Renewal of marriage vows by the guests

Following the marriage vows recited by the bride and groom, the officiant may ask all married couples to stand and renew their marriage vows. The officiant prompts the husbands and wives as they look into each others' eyes and renew their vows. This is especially touching for a Valentine's Day or New Year's wedding. I've witnessed this type of vows renewal ceremony many times, and it can be extremely touching.

> During a Greek Orthodox wedding ceremony, the best man places two crowns joined by a ribbon on the heads of the couple. Then he switches the crowns three times, symbolizing the holy trinity.

CHAPTER ELEVEN
ORIGINAL VOWS

One of the greatest rewards of being a writer of self-help books is receiving encouraging letters from my readers. Often these letters tell how the couple met, fell in love, and planned their weddings, in addition to enclosing copies of the vows or toasts composed with the help of my books. I thought you would enjoy reading the original wedding vows composed by and sent to me from two very special couples.

> *The significance of the modern wedding cake is said to have evolved from the Roman pastry of the "conferreatio," a cake that was broken on top of the bride's head as a symbol of fertility and fruitfulness.*

James and Katherine

Judge: *"James and Katherine, because of your love and faith in each other, today your lives will have a new beginning. Every experience you have ever had, everything you have ever done, and everything you have ever learned has brought you to this moment, when you stand before family and friends to take each other as husband and wife. You each bring your individual strengths and weaknesses, hopes and fears to this marriage, but as you confront the future as a married couple,* may you complement each other, support and strengthen one another. May you grow together in love and trust, sharing your dreams, your adventures, your quiet times, through all the years of your married life.

"James, do you take Katherine to be your wedded wife, to share your life with her openly and honestly from this day forward? Will you love her, comfort her, honor and cherish her, for richer, for poorer, in sickness and in health, in joy and in sorrow, and be true and loyal to her as long as you both shall live?"

In Great Britain, it is still considered to be good luck when a black cat crosses a bride's path on her way to the ceremony.

James: "I do."

Judge: "Katherine, do you take James to be your wedded husband, to share your life with him openly and honestly from this day forward? Will you love him, comfort him, honor and cherish him, for richer, for poorer, in sickness and in health, in joy and in sorrow, and be true and loyal to him as long as you both shall live?"

Katherine: "I do."

Judge: "Please join hands and repeat: I James/Katherine, take you Katherine/James as my beloved wife/husband. I promise to love and respect you always, and to be a patient husband/wife, honest and trusting. I promise to walk by your side through life as your best friend, your sweetheart, your helpmate, in good times and in bad, and to work hard at keeping our marriage healthy. I promise that my love will stay true and strong for all time, even as we grow old together."

Judge: (ring vows, repeated after the judge) *"James/Katherine, I offer this ring as a symbol of my love and my commitment to you. Wear it always as a reminder, to you and to the world, that I have chosen you above all other men/women, and that, from this day forward, you are my husband/wife."*

Paul and Paulette

Paulette wrote, *"Our marriage is so unique. We dated when we were young, at ages 25 and 32. That didn't work out and neither of us married. Then, when we bumped into each other 19 years later, we married when he was 52 and I was two months short of 46, and we are still the oldest first-time bride and groom we have heard of where neither had been married before. And it's been wonderful."*

Paulette went on to say that on their 10th wedding anniversary she wanted them to repeat their wedding vows, but that Paul thought the idea was a little off the wall, until he read my book, *Complete Book of Wedding Vows,* which includes a chapter filled with reaffirmation vows. He read the book and loved the idea. Paul and Paulette crafted their vows together. Here are their poignant reaffirmation vows which were exchanged on their 10th wedding anniversary:

Paul: *"Dearest Paulette, tonight, as we reaffirm our wedding vows, I commit my life to you anew, and I vow to continue to be a loving, true, and faithful husband, as long as we both shall live."*

Paulette: *"Dearest Paul, ours has been an incredible love story since the beginning. After both of us had given up hope that we would ever find the right person, I not only found the right man, but one so wonderful and so special."*

Paul: *"And I, too, have been so lucky to find a woman as wonderful as you. And to be in a marriage that has become more perfect each day, as we grow more and more in love with each other as each year goes by."*

Paulette: *"Our lives have been rich beyond measure, and today in the company of our beloved friends and family, I freely and publicly reaffirm my wedding vows. Especially the part in which we took each other, not only as husband and wife, but as best friends."*

Paul: *"And I promise with all my heart to love and cherish you, my best friend and lover, for all the blessed days God may yet allow us to live together on this earth. You are still my bride, my precious, beautiful one."*

Paulette: *"You are the most wonderful and unselfish person that I have had the joy and luck to know. I consider it an honor to have been married to you for 10 years. Throughout this time, I have fallen in love with you again hundreds of times for dozens of different reasons. I think of the years that still lie ahead and I can think of nothing more wonderful than that I will share them with you."*

Paul: *"I am proud to be your husband and pledge myself to you again this night with a love as fresh as the day I married you. Though we are in a secular place, may we take this opportunity to celebrate this day with two prayers, one a very special one because in it we thank God for bringing us to this day."*

"Baruch Atoy Adonai Elohainu Melech Ha-Olam, Borei P'ree HaGafen. And the blessing in English, which means 'We thank God for keeping us in life, sustaining us, and enabling us to reach this day.'"

Paulette: *"And now, in English, my vows, which I reaffirm, I,*

Paulette, take you, Paul, once again to be my lawfully wedding husband, and best friend, to love, comfort and honor you, in sickness and in health, in sorrow and in joy, so long as we both shall live."

Paul: "And I, Paul, take you, Paulette, once again to be my lawfully wedding wife, and best friend, to love, comfort, and honor you, in sickness and in health, in sorrow and in joy, so long as we both shall live."

It's a Dutch tradition for a bride to carry a handkerchief on her wedding day to catch her tears. This handkerchief is kept and given to her eldest daughter for good luck.

$\mathcal{E}$PILOGUE

You may help yourself to any of the vows or phrasings in this book; they are yours for the taking to mix and match at will. Or you may want to combine some of the phrasings found here with other prose or poetry you have gleaned from a love note or card received from your intended, or from your favorite love song or poem.

If you're searching for classical ideas and you didn't find exactly what you're looking for in Chapter 9, you may wish to consider other writings by these authors:

Elizabeth Barrett Browning
Anne Morrow Lindbergh
James Russell Lowell
E.E. Cummings
Carl Sandburg
John Keats
Anne Bradstreet
Charles Dickens
Wendell Berry
William Penn
Henry Van Dyke
John Donne
Stephen Sondheim

Robert Browning
Kahlil Gibran
John Ciardi
Gerard Manley Hopkins
James Joyce
Percy Bysshe Shelley
Christopher Marlowe
Walt Whitman
Philip Sidney
Mark Twain
Robert Burns
Martin Luther
William Shakespeare

As you compose your vows, however, whether they are contemporary or classical, consider these four questions:

- ❖ How do we feel about our unique relationship to each other?

- ❖ What are our hopes and dreams for our marriage?

- ❖ What words can we use to express these thoughts?

- ❖ Do we prefer monologue, dialogue, or the question and answer format ?

Your vows should reflect the deep emotional and spiritual bond between the two of you and the uniqueness of your own special relationship, which is like none other. Have fun as you create your own wedding vows!

I will be updating this book in the years to come, and I would appreciate a copy of your original wedding vows, if you would agree to share them with me. Please write to me in care of my publisher:

Diane Warner
c/o Career Press, Inc.
PO Box 687
Franklin Lakes, NJ 07417

$\mathcal{B}$IBLIOGRAPHY

Batts, Sidney F. *The Protestant Wedding Sourcebook*. Louisville, Ky.: John Knox Press, 1993.

Cole, Harriette. *Jumping the Broom: The African-American Wedding Planner*. New York: Henry Holt and Co., 1995.

Cotner, June. *Wedding Blessings*. New York: Broadway Books, 2003.

Crockett, Laura. *The Booke of Betrothal*. Mineola, N.Y.: Dover Publications, 2000.

Diamant, Anita. *The New Jewish Wedding*. New York: Simon and Schuster, 1993.

Glusker, David and Peter Misner. *Words for Your Wedding*. New York: HarperCollins, 1993.

Jones, Leslie. *Happy Is the Bride the Sun Shines On*. New York: Contemporary Books, 1995.

Kingma, Daphne Rose. *Weddings from the Heart.* York Beach, Maine: Conari Press, 1995.

Klausner, Abraham J. *Weddings: A Complete Guide to All Religious and Interfaith Marriage Services.* Royersford, Pa.: Alpha Publishing, 1986.

Latner, Helen. *Your Jewish Wedding.* New York: Doubleday & Co., 1985.

Leviton, Richard. *Weddings by Design.* San Francisco: Harper, 1993.

Matthews, Bette. *Wedding Toasts and Vows.* New York: Michael Friedman Publishing Company, 2001.

Mbiti, John S. *African Religions and Philosophy.* New York: Heineman, 1969.

Munro, Eleanor. *Wedding Readings.* New York: Penguin Books USA, 1986.

Naylor, Sharon. *Your Special Wedding Vows.* Naperville, Ill.: Sourcebooks, Inc, 2004.

O'Donohue, John. *Anam Cara: A Book of Celtic Wisdom.* New York: Perennial Publishing, 1998.

Ronatree Green, Danita. *Broom Jumping: A Celebration of Love.*
    New York: Entertaining Ideas, Ltd., 1992.

Smith, Susan. *Wedding Vows.* New York: Warner Books, Inc. 2001.

Younkin, Marty. *A Wedding Ceremony to Remember.* New York:
    Brown Books, 2003.

$\mathcal{A}$LSO BY DIANE WARNER

Published by Career Press:

Contemporary Guide to Wedding Etiquette

Best Wedding Ever

Complete Book of Wedding Toasts, 2nd edition

Complete Book of Wedding Showers

Complete Book of Baby Showers

Diane Warner's Wedding Question & Answer Book

Diane Warner's Big Book of Parties

Diane Warner's Complete Book of Children's Parties

Diane Warner's Great Parties on Small Budgets

Published by John Wiley Publishing:

Single Parenting for Dummies (co-authored with Marion Peterson)

Published by F & W Publications, Betterway Books:

How to Have a Big Wedding on a Small Budget, 4th edition

Big Wedding on a Small Budget Planner and Organizer

How to Have a Fabulous, Romantic Honeymoon on a Budget

Beautiful Wedding Decorations and Gifts on a Small Budget

Picture-Perfect, Worry-Free Weddings

How to Have a Great Retirement on a Limited Budget

Published by Pentan Overseas, Inc. (Books on Tape)

The Perfect Wedding Planner

Also by Diane Warner

Published by JISTWorks, Inc.

The Unauthorized Teacher's Survival Guide, 3rd Edition

The Inside Secrets of Finding a Teaching Job, 3rd Edition

Published by Accent Books, David C. Cook Publishing:

Puppets Help Teach

Puppet Scripts for Busy Teachers

$\mathcal{I}$NDEX

Adams, John Quincy, 55
Ado, the, 102
African-American handfasting, 188
American Lutheran vows, 23
Amish tradition, 183
apron dance, 193
Aramaic vows, 15
arranged marriage, 9–10
Arras, 31
Assyrian tradition, 129
autumn, 140
Av, 151
Aztec Indian, 161
Baby Boomers, 31
Bavarian tradition, 71
Bedi, 21
Belgian tradition, 95
Berry, Wendell, 201
Black cat, 196
Blessing stones, 191–193
Blossoms, 96
Blossoms, orange, 55, 184
Bowing, 107
Bradstreet, Anne, 174, 201
braids, 55
Braveheart, 182–183
bread, loaves, of, 99
bridal costume, Roman, 10–11
bride's processional, 66

British tradition, 186, 196
broom ceremony, jumping the, 191
broom, 146, 174
Browning, Elizabeth, 156, 162, 171, 201
Browning, Robert, 201
Buddha, 22
Buddhist handfasting ceremony, 188
Buddhist tradition, 22, 56
Burns, Robert, 152, 201
butterflies, 68
cake, wedding, 195
Calvin, John, 23
capture, marriage by, 10, 93
Carpatho-Russian Orthodox vows, 21
cat, black, 196
Catholic ring vows, 130–131
Catholic/Jewish vows, 123
Catholic/non-Catholic vows, 123
Celtic wedding ceremony, 182–183
ceremony,
  African handfasting, 188
  Buddhist handfasting, 188
  Celtic wedding, 182–183
  Christian handfasting, 189
  circle of acceptance, 74
  covenant wedding, 186–194
  double-ring, 16
  family medallion, 73–74
  family unity candle, 75

ceremony *(cont.)*,
    handfasting, 187–189
    Hindu handfasting, 188
    jumping the broom, 191
    Latino handfasting, 188
    Mexican handfasting, 188
    Renaissance, 183–184
    rose covenant, 186–187
    san-san-kudi, 104
    Victorian, 184–185
    wine, 93–94
Ch'ing Dynasty, 68
childhood sweethearts, vows, 53–54
chimney sweep, 132
Chinese,
    tea ceremony, 36
    tradition, 27, 36, 68, 115, 147
Chippewa Indian, 161
Christian,
    handfasting ceremony, 189
    ministry, vows, 120–121
Christmas Day wedding, 177–178
Chuppah, 73
Church of England, 22
Ciardi, John, 201
circle of acceptance ceremony, 74
civilization,
    Greek, 10
    Roman, 10
classics, vows inspired by the, 147–174
coins, 31
Colossians, Book of, 160
conferreatio, 195
congregational,
    blessing, 75–76
    Christian Church, 24
contract, marriage, 50, 87
Costa Rican tradition, 64
costume, Roman bridal, 10–11
Council of Trent, 10

covenant,
    ceremony, 187–189
    ceremony, rose, 186–187
    of salt, 193
    of salt, ring vows, 142–145
    of sand, 193
    wedding ceremony, 186–194
Cres, 74
crushing glass, 103
Cummings, E.E., 201
dance, apron, 193
Dickens, Charles, 153, 201
disregard for tradition, 31
Donne, John, 153, 201
double-ring ceremony, 16
dress, white, 15
drinking rituals, 147
ducks, 94
Duke Albert, 84
Duke of Edinburgh, 61
Dutch tradition, 19, 199
Eastern Orthodox vows, 19, 21
Ecclesiastes, Book of, 158
Egyptian tradition, 129
embroidered handkerchief, 95
Empress Eugenie, 15
English tradition, 96, 132
Ephesians, Book of, 159–160
Episcopalian,
    declaration of intent, 121
    ring vows, 131
    vows, 22–23
European tradition, 146
Evangelical Reformed Church, 24
Evangelical Lutheran ring vows, 131
family,
    medallion ceremony, 73–74
    members, 189–190
    unity candle ceremony, 75
favors, 137

214

fertility, 42, 89, 191, 195
Filipino tradition, 22, 42, 100
Finnish tradition, 83, 191
flora, 74
flower petals, 149
flowers, pikaki, 90
Franklin, Benjamin, 151
fruitfulness, 195
garlic, 146
Gautoma Buddha, 22
Genesis, Book of, 157
German tradition, 169
Gibran, Kahlil, 150-152, 169-171, 201
glass, crushing, 103
godparents, Mexican, 109
Great Plains Indian, 161
Greek,
    civilization, 10
    Orthodox tradition, 194
    Orthodox vows, 19
    tradition, 66, 67
guests,
    commitment by, 189-190
    renewal of vows by, 194
hand tying, 187
handfasting ceremony,
    African-American, 188
    Buddhist, 188
    Christian, 189
    covenant, 187-189
    Hindu, 188
    Latino, 188
    Mexican, 188
    wording for, 189
handkerchief, 118, 199
handkerchief, embroidered, 95
harvest, 140, 170
Haskell, Mary, 169-171
Hasthagranthi, 188
Hawaiian tradition, 90

hay cart, 71
Hebrews, Book of, 160
Hellen, Mary, 55
Hindu,
    handfasting ceremony, 188
    tradition, 28
    vows, 20-21
hoke of matrimony, 64
honey moon, 175
honey, wine and, 175
Hopi tradition, 76
Hopkins, Gerald Manley, 201
Indian tradition, 149
Indians, 161
intent, Episcopalian declaration of, 121
interfaith weddings, 122-128
Irish,
    lace, 38
    tradition, 38, 170
Isaiah, Book of, 160
Islam vows, 20
Islamic tradition, 131
Japanese tradition, 104
Javanese tradition, 77
Jerusalem, Jewish Temple in, 103
Jewish ring vows, 129-130
Jewish,
    Temple in Jerusalem, 103
    tradition, 30, 87, 128, 151, 156
    vows, 15-18
Jewish/Christian,
    interfaith vows, 123
    ring vows, 133
John, Book of, 160
Joyce, James, 154, 201
jumping the broom ceremony, 191
June, 80
Juno, 80
Keats, John, 171-172, 201
Kenyan tradition, 55

Ketubah, 87
kiss, wedding, 138
kneeling pillow, 109
Knot of Hercules, 10
Korean tradition, 94, 107
lace, Irish, 38
Latino handfasting ceremony, 188
Lindbergh, Anne Morrow, 201
Lowell, James Russell, 201
Luther, Martin, 23, 151, 201
Lutheran vows, American, 23
Maia, 74
Mala, 188
Mark, Book of, 157
Marlowe, Christopher, 201
marriage,
    arranged, 9-10
    by capture, 10, 93
    contract, 50, 87
marriages, vows for second, 55-66
matrimony, hoke of, 64
Matthew, Book of, 160
Messianic Jew/Christian, 124-128
Methodist ring vows, 132
Methodist vows, 24
Mexican,
    godparents, 109
    handfasting ceremony, 188
    tradition, 102, 109, 155
Mien wedding, 134
Ministry, vows of the, 120-121
Modedas, 31
Moroccan tradition, 140
myrtle, 84
Napoleon III, 15
Native American verses, 160-162
nature theme weddings, 178-181
Navajo Indian tradition, 178

New Year's Day wedding, 177
Nigerian tradition, 55
Night Among the Pines, A, 153
Nondenominational,
    Protestant vows, 26-30
    ring vows, 133-140
nontraditional wedding vows, 31-55
nuptial tie, 22
Eskimo Indian, 162
older couples, vows for, 95-102
orange blossoms, 55, 184
orchids, 68
original wedding vows, 195-199
outdoor weddings, 178
parchment scroll, 184
Passover, 151
Penn, William, 153, 201
Pennsylvania Dutch tradition, 174
period weddings, 182
Peter, Book of, 160
pikaki flowers, 90
Polish tradition, 50, 193
pomegranate, 68, 89
Prayer book, 109
prayer, vows based on, 121
Presbyterian,
    ring vows, 131
    vows, 23-24
Prince Albert, 15
Princess Elizabeth, 61
Pronuba, 11
prosperity, 42
Protestant,
    prayer, vows based on, 121
    vows, 26-30
Proverbs, Book of, 160
Quaker vows, 25-26
Queen Victoria, 15, 184

Rabbinical Assembly of America, 16
reaffirmation,
    service, 146
    service, classical vows for, 162
    vows, 77–94, 197
Reformation, 23
religious variations, vows with, 103–128
Renaissance ceremony, 183–184
renewal of vows by guests, 194
rice cake, 47
ring vows, 129–146
rings, 128, 144
rituals, drinking, 147
Roman,
    bridal costume, 10–11
    Catholic vows, 18–19
    civilization, 10
    tradition, 74, 138, 175
Romans, Book of, 160
rose covenant ceremony, 186–187
Rumi, Jalal Al-Din, 162
Russian Orthodox vows, 19
Russian tradition, 99
Ruth, Book of, 158
saké, 104
salt,
    covenant of, 193
    ring vows with, 142–145
sand, covenant of, 193
sandals, 129
Sandburg, Carl, 201
san-san-kudi ceremony, 104
Scripture, vows based on, 156–160
scroll, parchment, 184
second marriages, vows for, 55–66
Sefirah, 151
service, reaffirmation, 146
Seven Steps, ritual of, 21

Seven Wedding Blessings, 143
Shakespeare, 148–149, 162–168, 177, 201
Shavout, 151
Shelley, Percy Bysshe, 201
shoes, 129
    wooden, 19
Sidney, Philip, 201
significance of wedding cake, 195
Sondheim, Stephen, 201
Song of Solomon, Book of, 160
Song of the Open Road, 173
Sonnets from the Portuguese, 156, 173
Sonnets, Shakespeare's, 162–168
Spanish tradition, 31
spring, 74
Stevenson, Robert Louis, 153
stones, ceremony of wishing, 191–193
Swiss tradition, 118
Tammuz, 151
tea ceremony, Chinese, 36
Thali, 38
theme wedding vows, 175–194
Three Weeks, 151
Tibetan tradition, 47
Timbangan ritual, 77
To My Dear and Loving Husband, 174
tradition,
    Amish, 183
    Assyrian, 129
    Bavarian, 71
    Belgian, 95
    British, 186, 196
    Buddhist, 22
    Buddhist, 56
    Chinese, 27, 36, 68, 115, 147
    Costa Rican, 64
    disregard for, 31
    Dutch, 19, 199

tradition *(cont.)*,
    Egyptian, 129
    English, 96, 132
    European, 146
    Filipino, 22, 42, 100
    Finnish, 83, 191
    German, 169
    Greek Orthodox, 194
    Greek, 66, 67
    Hawaiian, 90
    Hindu, 28
    Hopi, 76
    Indian, 149
    Irish, 38, 170
    Islamic, 131
    Japanese, 104
    Javanese, 77
    Jewish, 30, 73, 87, 128, 143, 151
    Kenyan, 55
    Korean, 94, 107
    Mexican, 102, 109, 155
    Moroccan, 140
    Navajo Indian, 178
    Nigerian, 55
    Pennsylvania Dutch, 174
    Polish, 50, 193
    Roman, 74, 138, 175
    Russian, 99
    Spanish, 31
    Swiss, 118
    Tibetan, 47
    Welsh, 84, 165
traditional wedding vows, 15–30
Twain, Mark, 153, 201
Unitarian vows, 25
Unitarian/Universalist ring vows, 133
United Church of Canada vows, 132
United Church of Christ vows, 24
unity candle ceremony, family, 75

Valentine's Day wedding, 175–177
Valery, Paul, 154
Van Dyke, Henry, 201
verses, Native Americans, 160–162
Victorian ceremony, 184–185
Voltaire, 151
vows for,
    child sweethearts, 53–54
    older couples, 95–102
    second marriages, 55–66
    Christian ministry, 120–121
    reaffirmation service, 162–174
vows,
    American Lutheran, 23
    Aramaic, 15
    Carpatho-Russian, 21
    Catholic/non-Catholic, 123
    Eastern Orthdox, 19, 21
    Episcopalian, 22–23
    Greek Orthodox, 19
    Hindu, 20–21
    Islam, 20
    Jewish, 15–18
    Jewish/Catholic, 123
    Methodist, 24
    Nondenominational, 26–30
    nontraditional wedding, 31–55
    original wedding, 195–199
    Presbyterian, 23–24
    Quaker, 25–26
    reaffirmation, 77–94, 197
    renewal of guests', 194
    ring, 129–146
    Roman Catholic, 18–19
    Russian Orthodox, 19
    theme wedding, 175–194
traditional wedding, 15–30
Unitarian, 25
United Church of Christ, 24

wedding,
- cake, significance of, 195
- ceremony, Celtic, 182
- ceremony, covenant, 186
- ceremony, Renaissance, 183
- ceremony, Victorian, 184
- Christmas Day, 177
- favors, 137
- march, 186
- Mien, 134
- New Year's Day, 177
- Valentine's Day, 175–177
- interfaith, 122-128
- nature theme, 178-181
- outdoor, 178
- period, 182

Welsh tradition, 84, 165
Wesley, Charles, 24
Wesley, John, 24
white dress, 15
White House, 55
Whitman, Walt, 173, 201
windmill, 19
wine ceremony, 93–94
wine, 143, 147, 175
wine, honey and, 175
wishing stones, ceremony of the, 191-193
wooden shoes, 19
wording for handfasting ceremony, 189
Zeus, 67

About the Author

Diane Warner has authored more than 20 books and is nationally respected as one of America's finest authorities on weddings and parties. Her bestselling books include *Complete Book of Wedding Toasts, Complete Book of Wedding Vows, Complete Book of Wedding Showers, Complete Book of Baby Showers, Complete Book of Children's Parties, Diane Warner's Big Book of Parties,* and *How to Have a Big Wedding on a Small Budget.*

Diane Warner also writes for newspapers, magazines, and Websites; conducts seminars; and regularly appears on national television, including HGTV, the Discovery Channel, and CNN. She has two grown children and currently lives with her author-husband in Tucson, Arizona.